Legends Of The Boyne
And Selected Prose

The Tomb of Sir Lucas Dillon, at Newtown, near Trim.

A prayer to Muiredach, *"by whom this cross was made,"*
(west face) Monasterboice

FRANCIS LEDWIDGE

Legends Of The Boyne

and Selected Prose

Researched and edited by Liam O'Meara

RIPOSTE BOOKS DUBLIN

2006

First Published by *RIPOSTE BOOKS,* 2006
28 Emmet Rd Dublin 8. Ireland

ISBN: 1 901596 12 5

Printed by Enprint
© This selection and format, Liam O'Meara

Acknowledgements

Inchicore Ledwidge Society, especially Michael O'Flanagan; Joe
Ledwidge, nephew of the poet; Lord and Lady Dunsany; Ulick
O'Connor; the staff of the National Library of Ireland; the British
Library, Newspaper Archive, Colindale, London; the Library of
Congress, Washington D.C; Noel Ross, Co. Louth Archaeological
& Historical Society; Paul Murphy; the Drogheda Independent;
Frances Tallon of Meath County Library for pp 38; Vincent
Mulvany, Meath Archaeological and Historical Society for pp 70;
the family of the late Nancy Farrelly, photo pp116; Review of
Reviews, 1915, pp130; pp 141, is a *Punch* satirical cartoon, 1846-
the Hulton Archive/ Getty Images. Kenneth MacGowan and
Kamac Publications for use of other photographic material used in
this book. The engravings are from O'Hanlon's, *Lives of the Irish
Saints.*

Cover
Front: St. Patrick's Church, Slane, early twentieth century hand
tinted photograph: the Irish Historical Picture Centre, Dublin.
Back: Michael, Francis and Mrs. Ann Ledwidge with hackney
driver, Christy Cassidy at Janeville, Irish Life magazine, 1917.

Contents

Dedicated to the memory
of the late John de Courcy Ireland
Maritime historian and humanitarian

John wrote to me in 1997:

'Last night I went through the ritual that I operate twice a year of rereading all the Ledwidge poems I have. Of course he should be upgraded. I would not put him second even to Yeats myself.'

John passed away in the Spring of 2006 at the age of 93 years, as I was preparing this book for publication. He was a personal friend of my Grand Uncle, Jack Fitzgerald, Labour councillor and Lord Mayor of Dalkey and was present at his funeral in 1966- Editor.

Illustrations

The Sorrow of Drumree

(To the Memory of Francis Ledwidge)

There was no song of linnet
Nor voice in any tree,
When dawn, with silver trumpet
Was herald to Drumree;
No fish leapt in the river,
The red fox kept his lair
The spirits of the hedgerows
Were silent everywhere.
No boy passed softly whistling
With light foot o'er the dew
Meath larks forgot their matins,
No hymn came from the yew.
And to the quiet people
He'll chant his verse no more.
So let them talk of Flanders
And dead men by its shore.
That August day to twilight
The groves held reverie —
Then timid sang the blackbird
The sorrow of Drumree.'

Seumas O'Kelly, 1919
Editor, Sinn Fein

Omitted from O'Kelly's '*Ranns and Ballads,'* this version was never before published. Another, with slight variation was published in the Sunday Independent, in Feb. 1919.

Foreword

There are many beautiful portraits of the Boyne river and districts from which I could have chosen to use as an illustration for this book. Instead, I opted for a well worn hand-tinted photograph of the Roman Catholic church of Slane, taken and coloured at the turn of the last century. The story of this church with its detached belfry is covered in the essay on Slane in the series of Francis Ledwidge's, 'Legends of the Boyne.' The belfry is also the,

'...octagon spire toned smoothly down'

referred to in the poem 'Behind the Closed Eye'; the octagon being the old name for part of the village of Slane.

Ledwidge was a labourer of Meath and, like the children shown in this quaint picture, he grew up listening to the old legends, colourful history and folklore of his native village and surrounding areas. When he reached adulthood he made a bit of a name for himself locally when he retold some of these stories, bringing to them his own distinctive style and poetic touch. Originally titled *Legends and Stories of the Boyne-Side,* the articles began to appear weekly in the *Drogheda Independent*, beginning in November 1913 and ending in February 1914. The paper also intended to publish the stories in booklet form, but this idea was abandoned when the series came to an abrupt halt. A proof copy with pages yet uncut has survived and is today in the possession of the Co. Louth Archaeological and Historical Society, who very kindly loaned me the work for my perusal.

At this time Ledwidge was unemployed following his departure from the Meath Labour Union where he had held the position of secretary. He applied to the *Drogheda Independent* for some journalistic work and editor, Mr. Casey's reply of 'no vacancy' is said to have soured relations between them. Hence the sudden and absolute end to the series. The editor, however, showed that there was no animosity on his part by continuing to publish the poems as well as readers' letters and appreciative articles in praise of the 'New Poet.' It is possible that it was simply his rise to fame as a poet at this time that caused the diversion away from prose.

Ledwidge was a founding member of the Meath Labour Union, then only the second branch of its kind in the county. Within a short time it had spread to 15 areas and eventually 22. He was a very active member, championing the cause of the farm labourers. It was when the Union became an Approved Society that Frank secured the post of secretary and was given a little office at the back of Loughran's butcher's shop in Navan. Today he is commemorated at SIPTU's new premises in Navan, The Dan Shaw Centre, where the main hall is named after him and an artistic presentation consisting of three glass panels showing aspects of his life and works greets the visitor at the foyer.

Numerous commentators on the life of Ledwidge have dipped into *Legends and Stories of the Boyne-Side* because of the fascinating glimpses which he has given us, here and there, of his personal life. Indeed, when biographer Alice Curtayne came to write her *Life of the Poet,* she relied heavily on these and the autobiographical letter to Lewis Chase. Some of her other sources were, as she confessed in one of her notebooks, statements from elderly people of 'uncertain memory.'

While the 'Legends', collected here for the first time are the main focus of this book, I have included also, some earlier uncollected work, a sample of his short stories. 'The Wheel of Fortune,' is a tale of the land, landlordism and emigration, the other is the creepy 'Dark Sisters of Barristown.'

It was John Cassidy, the renowned Meath sculptor and former student of Slane National School, where Frank had later attended, who urged him to find a patron for his art. This was possibly the most invaluable advise that anyone ever offered to Francis Ledwidge. He immediately sent a copybook of verse to Lord Dunsany and there ensued an unlikely, but very genuine friendship between 'the peer' and the 'peasant poet.' Dunsany was a leading figure in the Golden Age revival of Irish literature, who would live to be the author of over 500 short stories and who would see some of his plays running simultaneously in London, Paris, Moscow and New York. Soon, the work of his young protégé began to appear in the most respected of London's literary magazines. I am therefore glad to be able to include here, Frank's own little tribute to John Cassidy, an amusing pen portrait displaying some of the writer's journalistic aspirations.

Ledwidge, no doubt with his Lordship's advice, underwent a change of image: he took to carrying a walking cane and wearing a broad hat; he allowed his hair to grow long and began wearing a flowing bow-tie. The finishing touch was the rimless round spectacles which he wore of necessity. This, was how he was presented to the public in the Spring of 1914, when Lord Dunsany gave his introductory lecture at the National Literary Society. As a result of this introduction Ledwidge became an established figure on the poetry circuit. His celebrity status was evident when a reporter and a photographer arrived at the family home in Janeville. The back cover of this book shows Frank with his brother Michael and Mrs. Ann Ledwidge; also, Christopher Cassidy, the local cab driver waiting to take the pair back to Beauparc.

No one who has read these historical accounts from Ledwidge's perspective can be in any doubt as to the writer's feelings on Irish nationalism. Nationalism, to most people at that time meant Home Rule. Ledwidge was a staunch advocate of Home Rule and as founder member of the Slane branch of the Irish Volunteers was ready to lay down his life in any armed conflict with the Ulster Volunteers who had threatened to oppose the enforcement of the Act. He did not, however, feel that the Home Rule issue should be used as a reason for Irish participation in the Great War. That was not the reason the young local men under his charge had joined the Volunteers. Nor was he persuaded by the reassurances given to Redmond. It was of no consequence what the British offered, no matter how sincere, as long as the Ulster Volunteers were still determined to hold firm: *"Home Rule is as far off now as ever,"* he told the packed assembly gathered to vote on the issue. He voted against the proposal on a matter of principal, though on a personal level he was appalled at the plight of the smaller nations and believed that the Germans had to stopped. We know this from a poignant poem of his published the following year in the *Sprig of Shillelagh*, journal of the Royal Inniskilling Fusiliers:

'Tis the cry of the land made desolate
'Tis the wail of a wild despair,
In the flowing rain and the blowing rain,
Calls me from everywhere.

'Tis the rustle of golden harvest
Where the reapers and all are slain,
Fills the wood call with a blood call,
And to many calls in vain.

'Tis the cry of a woman childless,
'Tis the moan of a homeless woe,
That woos me and pursues me,
So I must arise and go.

('The Call,' January 1915)

Ledwidge joined the Inniskillings at Richmond Barracks, Goldenbridge (Inchicore) Dublin on the 29th. October 1914. He survived the Gallipoli landings and went to his second front with the 10th. Irish Division to Serbia and Greece in 1915. The following year he recorded his experiences there while recuperating from a gall-bladder infection in a hospital bed in Manchester. The account of 'The Battle of the Three Sheep,' appeared in the *Sunday Chronicle* on the 7th. May 1916, ironically the same week as the paper was reporting on the court-martials of the leaders of the Irish uprising, which were being held at Richmond Barracks, and of the subsequent executions of the first three prisoners, Padraic Pearse, Thomas MacDonagh and Thomas Clarke. It was an irony that was not lost on Ledwidge. He was deeply effected by the news and immediately began work on a new poem, one which would be considered by many people his greatest. It was titled simply, 'Thomas MacDonagh.'

According to Alice Curtayne, Ledwidge arrived back to the smoking ruins of Dublin City around about the 10th. May 1916. He returned to Richmond and then to Ebrington Barracks in Derry. Later that year the distraught and totally disillusioned soldier was sent to his third front, on the Franco-Belgian border. In June 1917, he received an enquiry from a university professor, Lewis Chase and replied with an extraordinary autobiographical letter which the professor received on the last day of June. A month later, almost to the day, Lance-Corporal Francis E. Ledwidge was killed by an exploding shell.

When Curtayne was writing her *Life of the Poet* she cleverly and skillfully broke the chain of this letter using sections of it throughout the book in the telling of the Ledwidge story. Unfortunately, however, the remaining large segment of the letter as it appears at the close of her book has lost its power. I was surprised to find also, that when the letter originally appeared in the *Century Magazine* in 1918, the section where Ledwidge is being less than deferential to W.B Yeats was omitted. Here then, perhaps for the first time, is the letter in its entirety, unabridged and continuous.

Ledwidge enthusiasts will discover in **Legends of the Boyne,** the man behind the poetry; his views on political as well as everyday things; his sense of humour, as shown in some of the biographical accounts, set against his moral outrage when writing on historical matters. But this book should appeal to a wider audience; those interested in the history and folklore of Royal Meath. The Meath of his time, which he compared with that of former years, is now itself part of that history. His naming of certain people, shops and details of landscape will be of particular interest in that regard. It will serve as an introduction for modern day readers to Ledwidge the prose writer. His status as a poet is well established, having being critically acclaimed by the likes of Walter de la Mare and Virginia Wolfe, and with many new admirers among today's leading poets, including Seamus Heaney.

We know that prior to becoming a soldier Francis Ledwidge was veering towards a career in journalism. I have no doubt, that had he survived the war, he would have developed his prose writing as much as his poetic skills. Alas, it was not to be; and the promise shown here illustrates, just as his poetry does, how great was that loss.

Liam O'Meara

The Boyne And Its Origin

'I'll sing tonight of a fairy land,
In the lap of the ocean set;
And of all the lands I've travelled o'er,
'Tis the loveliest I have met.
Where the roses creep and the willows weep,
And the balmy breezes blow;
In that dear old land, that green old land,
Where the lovely rivers flow.'

Thus ran the first verse of Father Ryan's most beautiful poem. And now that I have recalled it, my thoughts revert to the first time upon which I read it, and every circumstance of the day. With another companion I had been sent with cattle to the shipping at Drogheda, with sixpence in my pocket on which both of us were expected to make a meal, and in my head the pride of my commission. I remember with what logic we discussed the allocation of the silver piece, and how when my companion suggested changing it into coppers and making an even divide of it I endeavoured to reason with him the folly of such a proceeding by quoting something from 'Poor Richard,' which I now forget, but remember was not at all appropriate. But the sixpence was a source of great anxiety to me after all, and I think I was afraid of losing it, it was so small besides, six coppers would jingle in one's pocket when running to turn the cattle from a bye-way, and it was troublesome having to clasp the silver bit tight in your hand on such an occasion, as I thought I had better convert it into coppers at the half-way house. On intimating this to my companion he proposed we should buy a half ounce of tobacco and two clay pipes. To this I readily acquiesced, but it afterwards cost me a sick stomach and a black eye, and made me an inveterate lover of the brown weed. After shipping the cattle we sallied up the town, giddy, silent and sick, with three-pence-halfpenny deep in our exchequer; we had made friends again while doing a tour on the boat, because there was enmity in the heart of the Mell boys against any lad from the country, and only by our united forces could we hope to pass that quarter unscathed.

After disposing of three hours there was a halfpenny left, and for that I bought a green song book, which contained Father Ryan's beautiful poem, the first verse of which I quote above. How I spelled it until I could recite the first verse no one but myself knows now, for my companion has long since crossed to God. But a new trouble arose now like an eclipse on the beauty of the poem, for I had not been certain if the good priest had included the Boyne in his song as one of the lovely rivers of Ireland, and when I appealed to my companion he was likewise doubtful, so the only thing left me to do was to grow up and know. And many an evening while growing up I would wander by the river with a jealous fear in my heart that beyond the blue mountains of the distant South the rival of the Boyne sang down through broader and more fecund savannahs and with a more majestic sweep, and greater in story and song. And in my soul there swelled the seed of a great determination to rise up one day, and in defence of my own Boyne put that of the Southern priest's to shame. But when the discretion came I found I had been grossly in error, and had sinned against the rivers of the North and South. And I felt proud of the Boyne because it was greatest in story and song, and a little vexed that I had not been born a genius, and before Sir William Wilde and D'Arcy McGee, for the determination fostered in my youthful soul had been burgeoned into a beautiful flower that would not fade, for all that fate had cast me upon the downhill of the world. The present series of stories and legends are the gleanings of arduous years gathered from old books and the lips of wrinkled Seannichies, and it is the hope of the compiler that they may be a source of interest to the boys and girls of the Gaelic League whenever they are introduced. President Roosevelt has said that next to developing original writers in its own time, nothing can befall a nation more fortunate than to have revealed to it the writings of a buried past. While thanks to the literary activity born of the revival of the Gaelic League, we are fortunate in this, I fear that some of the most beautiful legends of our country are dying with the Seannichies. It is these, the least known, that I have been gathering, and while I hope they may be read by all, I dedicate them to the boys and girls aforementioned, because they are the men and women of the future, into whose hands our unfinished work must fall.

I take the Boyne as my ribbon, and travel by it from Roch Ramor to the sea, and at the most interesting places I shall tell their stories, in chronological order, from legend down to authentic history. But first let me tell you why the Boyne is so called, and how it came into existence.[1] Formerly there was but a small well, around which grew three magic hazel trees. These trees bore crimson nuts, and whoever ate them became possessed of all the knowledge of the world. But even the gods of the land were not permitted to approach this place, and only mentioned it with bowed heads around the sacrificial fires. But Boann, the wife of Dagda, whom we shall meet later, had heard how three salmon, which inhabited the well, ate always the nuts dropped into the water and were all-wise. With the proverbial curiosity of women, she stole secretly to the spot, but ere she reached it the waters arose and drove her away. She escaped, but the waters never returned, and the salmon left the well to search to the sea for the nuts of wisdom. One of these fish was afterwards caught by Finn Mac Cool near Slane, and its omniscience descended to him.

Thus it was that the Boyne came into existence and hence its name. Beautiful always, and calm, it slips across the shadows of great trees on its margins, sometimes slow and deep like a great mirror on the floor of a wood, sometimes shallow and noisy, stretching away like a silver scimitar gracefully into perspective. There, you hear it in the fields where a town makes noise, and again in the lea-lands, where the harvest sways or the cattle tread it in the heat of summer. At its appointed time the cuckoo tells its name to the hills across it, and the blackbird sings above it until dark. Here and there a tributary stream brawls into it and goes off in its arms to meet the tide at Drogheda. And there, the sea lends its power and depth, and little homing ships come in at twilight from the sea, or men with the wander-longing set off upon adventures.

---

[1] From the Book of Leinster

Clonard

**'A tower of gold over the sea
Is Finnian the fair, the beloved root
Of the great Cluain Iraird.'**
— From *The Calendar of Irish Saints.*

On a lovely morning in early May I stood upon the plains of Clonard in the company of one of the most illustrious poets of the age. A soft rain had fallen during the night, and a light vapour trembled above the fields like the exhalation of its flowers. The poppies, wakened from a long lethargy of drought burned like slow fires in the potato fields, and the blossom broke on the thorn like a light covering of snow. There was a Sabbath air about the whole scene, a Sabbath air full of song. We stood upon the Western bank of the Boyne, watching the brown trout leap in the noisy sharps, and a silent crane, as lonely as the fabled one of Isnaskea, and as rigid as if Perseus had just passed and showed him the Gorgon's head. He stood upon a large stone in mid-stream looking off at a tangent as if listening to the sharps above him, where the trout were.

We spoke little, for our thoughts had strayed far back upon the hilly leagues of time, when Partholon and his industrious followers fought with the Fomors, and slew their deformed and malevolent leader, Cichol the Footless. And I thought upon the slow method of Time, and how after centuries of incessant warfare with man and change, he comes silently into his own again. For the plain whereon we stood was but desert when Partholon first fought upon it, and yet desert when the angel led St. Finnian across it to Muiredach, sovereign of Hy-Kinsellagh. From that time forward until the reign of Henry V111, it was far famed for its schools of Literature, Art, Science, Philosophy and Theology. But today nothing but a token remains of the great monastery founded by St. Finnian, and but a small relic of the great abbey erected by Walter de Lacy as late as 1175. Again the desert stretches across it like a great doom, and over it all Time gloats as one who has won a great victory. The little village of Clonard is situated in the barony of Upper Moyfenrath, County of Meath, 11 miles from Kilcock, and 25 from Dublin. The original name of the place was 'Ross Finchuil,' the "place of the White Hazel." In the Annals of the Four Masters it is called 'Cluain Iraird,' "The retirement of the Western heights," or, according to O'Donovan, "Erard's Lawn."

But I must first tell you of the people of Partholon and the Fomors, of their famous battle, and the final end of the Partholian Race. Some historians write that the people of the Godless Danu were the first divine inhabitants of Ireland. But, according to eminent authorities on Celtic Mythology, in the dark backwark and abysm of time, there fell from the sky a God whom men call Partholon, and with him a retinue of twenty-four male and twenty-four females. It was on the first day of May, the day called 'Beltaine,' sacred to Bile, the God of Death.

At this remote period Ireland consisted only of one treeless, greenless plain, watered by two lakes and seven rivers. But as this divine race increased, the land widened under them like magic and the people laboured to make it arable and fit for habitation. The 'Fomors,' who were dwellers of the sea, sought to exterminate this industrious race, but in spite of all their wiles and treachery it had increased from forty-eight members to five thousand in the space of three hundred years, and the land grew from one treeless plain to four fecund provinces, and acquired seven new lakes. The Fomors were led by a huge deformed monster called 'Cichol the Footless,' who had tormented the Partholonians for three centuries. Partholon himself slew this semi-divine savage in a great pitched battle on the plains of Cluain Iraird, and for another three hundred years there was peace.

I cannot vouch for the geographical truth of this battle, for we read in the old legends that the Fomors never ventured far away from the water, and after the Partholonians had passed and the Tuatha De Danann ruled in the land they sought on several occasions to submerge it, so that the Tuatha De Danann were obliged to hide all the lakes of Ireland before engaging into combat with them.

But a doom fell upon the Partholonians that wasted them like icicles in the sun. Upon the first of May, the anniversary of their arrival, there began a mysterious epidemic which destroyed them all in a week. Foreseeing their end they gathered upon their first created plain, then called 'Sean Mag,' so that those who lived might easily bury those that died. Their graves are yet marked by a mound near Dublin called 'Tallaght' but formerly known as 'Tallaght Muintre Partholian,' "The Plague-grave of Partholon's People." Thus passed away the earliest race known in mythology, just as Nemed and her followers fought the Fomors in another part of the island. It would take too long to relate the compact of Nemed's people with the Fomors, and the destruction of their towers on Tory Island, besides, it would be quite irrelevant, so we must drop the curtain on the events of all those years and come down to St. Finnian the 'Tutor of Irish Saints.'

St. Finnian was born near the Barrow not far from New Ross. His father's name was Fintan, of the race of Loschain, that of his mother Taleck. They were said to have been Christians at the time of Finnian's birth. He was baptised by St. Abban and received his ecclesiastical education from the Bishop of Trim —Forthenn. At an early age he was sent to Tours, and on his return spent a considerable time at St. David's in Wales. During his stay here he founded three churches, and made the acquaintance of three distinguished Britons whose names occur in the ecclesiastical history of Ireland. They are David, Sildas, and Cadoc.

After spending some years at St. David's, he is said to have had a vision in which an angel showed him the place of his resurrection. Accompanied by some religious Britons who were much attached to him, he returned to Ireland about the year AD 515. He visited his friend Cayman at Dairinis, after which he landed at Kille Cairne, in the County of Wexford, and from thence he visited Muiredach, sovereign of Hy-Kinsellagh, to ask the prince's permission to speak the Gospel in his territory. Having obtained it, he established a religious community at a place called Achadabla, and another at Magna, in the district of Ho-barche. In this place he preached the Gospel for seven years, and on several occasions lectured before the nuns of St. Brigid. Historians differ as to the year St. Finnian came to Clonard. Harris, places this event at AD 520, Usher, at AD 544, and Dean Cogan at AD 530.

Clonard is said to have been a desert when St. Finnian founded his monastery, and by the labours of his monks was converted into a luxuriant soil. The monastery in a very short time became famous as a holy repository of all wisdom, and the most famous school in Europe. Its students at one time numbered three thousand youths, not only from Ireland, and Britain, but from Germany. Some of the greatest names in the annals of our country studied Scripture and Theology under St. Finnian of Clonard; St. Columcille, St. Kieran, the founder of Clonmacnoise; the venerable Kieran of Sagair; the great St. Brendan of Clonfert, and his namesake of Birr; St. Molua, the founder of Clonfert; St Canice after whom the city of Kilkenny is called; St. Columb of Tirdaglass, and hundreds of others were all enrolled as pupils of St. Finnian.

St Finnian lived a most austere life, his usual food being bread and herbs; his drink, water, except on festival days, when he drank a little whey, and sometimes ate fish. He was a profound commentator of the Scriptures and an untiring labourer in the Vineyard of Christ. The fame of his learning and good works spread over the world, and his hospitality was the theme of the wandering minstrel. The word 'stranger' was holy to him and the poor were his loving friends, and his most beloved. He clad the naked, sheltered the homeless and fed the hungry; yet for all his prodigality he was contented with bread and herbs, and for all that he rested the weary, he was himself never rested, his bed being a board and his pillow a stone. He was attended in his last illness by St. Columb, and died on the 12th. of December, 552 AD.

"Behold foreigners confiscating our property"
— Daniel O'Connell

In the year of Our Lord 1175 Walter de Lacy erected a monastery on the site of the ancient abbey of Clonard under the patronage of St. Peter. This monastery was richly endowed by De Lacy and other Anglo-Norman Knights, and here for the space of 367 years the monks of St. Augustine spread the faith, and kept the old traditions of St. Finnian alive. These monks became famous for their erudition, and kept a large school. Art was a second religion to them, and it was chronicled that their Scriptorium was known across the world. Nor did they allow the land to grow fallow, but most industriously tilled their nine hundred and twelve acres of arable land and tended their flocks on their thousand acres of pasture. This peaceful state of affairs continued until Henry the V111 assumed the supremacy of the English Church. You have all read with what impunity he plundered the sanctuary and what acts of vandalism his base mind willed.

In 1533, George Brown, an Englishman, was appointed to the archiepiscopal see of Dublin. The English novelties were resisted by Dr. Cromer, Archbishop of Armagh. Brown, finding the Irish people adamant, wrote to Cromwell telling him his mission had failed, and advising him to call a parliament which would order the unsheathing of the sword; and suggesting that the terrors of imprisonment, confiscation and death might frighten the Irish into the religion invented to meet the carnal desires of the English King. A Parliament was convened in 1536, and the first measure introduced was an act establishing the King as spiritual head of the Church.

To this was added an addendum prohibiting appeals to Rome, and stipulating that the first fruits should be paid to the King instead of to the Pope; and that the twentieth part of the annual profits of ecclesiastical promotions should fall to the crown. But the Reformation was making slow progress in Ireland after all, and his Majesty's rage made his deputies in Ireland tremble, and many a time he nodded, and every nod meant death. Thus he wrote to Brown in 1537:

"Such is your lightness in behaviour, and such is the elation of your mind in pride, that glorifying in foolish ceremonies, and delighting in 'We' and 'Us,' in your dream comparing yourself to a prince in honour and estimation, that all virtue and honesty is almost banished from you."[2]

Brown replied that his Majesty's letter made him tremble in body for fear of incurring his royal displeasure. The religious houses were all now suppressed, and in 1542 the King granted to Sir William Birmingham, the late monastery of Clonard, its church, belfry, cemetery, hall, and garden. And in 1551, Edward V1 granted to Sir Thomas Cusack its demesne, with the custom called 'towlbolla' in the town of Clonard; Kylreny, 60 acres, and the lands surrounding; Kylglass, Ballinluga, Toboyen, Kiltaylen, Kyllaghan, Clonedaly, Trym; to hold for ever in fee farm; rent £8 sterling.

Clonard is now no more. It passed away as Troy passed, but its story shall be with us for ever. It has been divided like the garments of Christ, and lots have been drawn for its treasures. The hemlock nods now where once the Saint prayed, and the cattle low where once the monk laboured. It's glory is now but a tale that is told and left away upon the shelves of time.

---

[2] Copies of State papers, modernized by Ledwidge.

Trim Castle

Trim

'O, not for thee the glow, the bloom,
Who changest not in any gale,
Nor branding summer suns avail
To touch thy thousand years of gloom.'

Trim is said to be an excellent example of an Irish county town. But whoever has said this did not mean the Trim of seven hundred years ago; not the Trim of story and romance, but rather the Trim of today—the Trim of the workhouse. Entering it from the Navan side, one is immediately struck by the absolute barrenness and the woe-begone appearance of the whole scene. The Boyne is at its worst here, running along the dirty back of a high wall, and stretching into wild open fields where I could not even see cattle. But the Trim of fourteen hundred years ago, and of seven hundred years ago was more inspiring, and remembering its story, one almost half expects to see Roderick O'Connor at the head of his 15,000 men come suddenly all green round the corner of a street.

Somebody from Miggins' hotel induced my companion to go fishing, and I was left to excavate the buried past alone among the lean ruins that tower above the town like starved sentinels of a besieged legion. I went to see the new Catholic church in the hopes of meeting the parish priest there, and learning from him the exact location of King Laoghaire's well, and the history of Our Lady of Trim. The new church is a magnificent edifice and a credit to the parish. I met Father Woods as I anticipated, and will not hesitate to say he is one of the finest types of the Soggarth Aroon I have ever met. I only wish we had more Father Woods's and more Father Barrys in Ireland, and if so we were a more contented, a happier, and a more Irish people. I was speaking to Father Woods for a few minutes and was about to tell him how I had seen two Candlemas Sundays this year, one in Slane, and one in Athboy the following week, but a poor woman was waiting for him at his door, and— well, Father Woods would not keep charity waiting, until the inquisitiveness of a nomad scribe was satisfied. I felt sorry for the old church pining there in its humility beside the new one. Its windows were broken and boarded up and it stands there neglected like an old faith. It seems to me the type God wants men to pray to Him in, but then the clergy argue about the beauty of Solomon's temple, and, as the priest who taught me to serve mass remarked — *"The priest, like a woman, always has the last word."* So I left the good priest administering charity to the poor woman and returned to the Yellow steeple, and sitting on a large stone there, I travelled back to prehistoric years on the rail-road of thought.

Trim is the only portion of County Meath mentioned in the Cuchulain Saga, it is there called Ath Truim, 'The Ford of the Alders,' and was the scene of King Connor's last battle with Maeve of Connaught. Cuchulain himself took no part in this battle he being then badly wounded, and wound in wicker full of grass at Dundealgan (Dundalk). This was the last battle of the 'Cattle Spoils of Cooley.' I shall tell you briefly how these battles commenced and ended. Maeve, King Ailill's wife, and Queen of Connaught, discovered one morning that her husband had one bull more than her in his pastures. Jealous of this she sent messengers to King Connor of the North requesting the loan of the brown bull of Cooley for a time. Connor was glad to have the opportunity of disappointing her, because she was his betrothed wife, and would not wed him because he would rule her; she was obstinate and proud and tossed Ailill to the throne of Connaught because she could sway him. Enraged at Connor's refusal to grant her request she mustered a large army and battles raged spasmodically between the North and the West for years.

Cuchulain, who was the Achilles of Ireland, performed many wonderful deeds at these battles, and often by himself kept the whole army of Maeve at bay. But at last he fell, wounded by the hand of a dear companion, and Maeve rifled the fields and drove the brown bull home. On hearing this, Connor pursued her, and Maeve, fore-warned, took her cattle and those of Ailill along with the brown bull of Cooley to Ath Truim, and there made a last stand against the forces of the North. But the brown bull of Cooley killed Ailill's white bull during the battle and then coughed up his own heart and died.

We hear no more of Trim then until Laoghaire was reigning at Tara, when it is said that a well bubbled up there in which Laoghaire's druids saw the coming of St. Patrick and the fall of the Crom Cruagh. The King, on being thus informed hied to the well, and having drunk, was filled with a great sadness, and prophesied of the water before a multitude the advent of one who, with water, would wash away the gods from the hearts of his people. This referred to the Sacrament of Baptism. I was not able to locate the well on my visit to Trim, but I believe this to be the same well in which Foirtchern, grandson of Laoghaire, was baptised by St. Loman. The baptism of Foirtchern is the earliest Christian reference made to Trim. Legend says that St. Patrick when on his holy navigation to Ireland, left St. Loman, his nephew, at the mouth of the Boyne in charge of his boat, instructing him to wait for him there forty days and nights. St. Loman waited eighty days for Patrick's return, and then in obedience to a divine command he faced his boat to the river and came against the stream as far as the 'ford of the alders.' And when it was morning, Foirtchern found him reciting the Gospel; and admiring it and the doctrine St. Loman preached was baptised by the Saint and remained with him until his guardian came to seek him. St. Loman remained with Foirtchern until St. Patrick returned, who, overjoyed at the good work his nephew had done, founded a church there. St. Loman died A.D. 482, and Foirtchern succeeded him as Bishop of Trim, but three days afterwards he resigned it to Cathald, who held the holy office until he died in the year of Our Lord 554.

In the year 1155, Trim and its churches were burned to the ground. After the English invasion, Trim became one of the principal strongholds of the Pale. De Lacy erected a military fort here in 1173, but Tyrell, his deputy, set fire to it in his absence, seeing the approach of Roderick O'Connor, King of Ireland, and the last King of Ireland.

De lacy, who was in England at this time, knew nothing of what had happened at Trim, and before his return, Tyrell had the fort rebuilt. In 1210, King John visited Trim, and remained there for some time. It is said he founded a monastery there, though some attribute this to the Plunkett family. In 1263 the Dominican Abbey was founded by Geoffrey de Joinville, who shortly afterwards went with the Crusaders to Palestine. This is the same Geoffrey de Joinville who was appointed Lord Justice of Ireland in 1273. In 1330 a flood rose in the Boyne which totally obliterated the town of Trim (then made of clay and wattles), swept away all the bridges, and did much harm to the monasteries of Trim and Drogheda. In 1399 Richard the Second confined the two sons of the Duke of Gloucester in the Castle of Trim; one of these, Henry, was afterwards Henry V. In 1447 Sir John Talbot, Lord Furnival, and the Earl of Shrewsburg held a Parliament at Trim and passed an act prohibiting any Englishman in Ireland from wearing a moustache after the fashion of the Irish. About this time in the abbey of St. Mary's, Trim, was a statue of the Blessed Virgin under which many miracles were wrought. Pilgrims flocked from all parts of the country to witness the many wonders enacted by 'Our Lady of Trim,' and in 1472 an Act of Parliament was passed at Naas granting to the friars of Trim, amongst other things, all the custom and services of the villeins of the manor of Trim, for the purpose of erecting a perpetual wax light before the image of the Blessed Virgin. When Henry V111, appointed Thomas Brown as reforming Archbishop of Dublin, Brown wrote thus to (Thomas) Cromwell in 1538:

"It is common among the Irish that I intend to pluck down 'Our Lady of Trim,' which I never intended, although my conscience would right well serve me to suppress such idols."[3]

But shortly afterwards, in the same year, with many other images the statue of the Blessed Virgin was burned, and if Brown had had any scruples in plucking it down, he had none in robbing the abbey of the gifts the pilgrims had brought there. Her image was sacrificed to the avarice of the Reformation, but devotion to her

---

[3] Copies of State papers, modernized by Ledwidge.

became more inflamed and the horror of the Iconoclasts more intensified. In the May of 1539, the satellites of Henry V111 summoned the Abbot and his community to surrender, and yielding to force those poor labourers of God were forced to sign their own expulsion. And, now, to enrich the coffers of their profligate King, they gutted the abbey, carrying away with them vases, jewels, ornaments of gold, altar linen, etc., to the value, it is stated, of £1,861. 15s. 2d. In 1542, the King granted the abbey, with all its appurtenances to Sir Anthony St. Ledger. All that now remains of St. Mary's Abbey is the Yellow Steeple. A small portion of its exquisite staircase may yet be seen. Its window, which must have been a veritable work of art, is almost gone. Nothing remains but its story, and let us hand that down to posterity.

The Dominican Friary

In the year 1263, a monastery for the illustrious Order of St.Dominick was erected beneath the Athboy Gate. On the Sunday next after the Feast of St. Matthew, the Archbishops of the Kingdom held a meeting here under the presidency of Armagh, and entered into a remarkable association for the promotion and strength of the Church. For over 250 years the monks of this Order laboured industriously for the propagation of the faith, never once deviating from the lines laid down 272 years previous. The fate of this monastery was that of St. Mary's; it was rifled by the vandals of the Reformation and divided amongst the perverts of the neighbourhood. After the dissolution of their monastery the friars lingered long in the neighbourhood, preaching the gospel in the face of much persecution, and still hoping on for better times.

The Grey Friary

The Grey Friary was founded by King John, or as some say by the noble family of Plunkett. Its fate was that of St. Mary's and the Dominican Friary. But after the spoliation of the monastery these settled in a more humble abode, and supported by the free offerings of the people ministered here until the inhuman edict of 1697, banished them from the country. Early in the eighteenth century the scattered brethren of this Order returned and founded the friary of Cortown, and for a century laboured in the service of God and His people. This is the story the ruins of Trim tell, let us listen to it, and while we forgive let us still remember. But before we leave Trim there is another sad story to tell; it is the massacre of men, women, and children by the Puritans in the years 1641-1642.

Trim In 1641-2
"To Your Tents, 0 Israel!"

It is not to be wondered at that when the Mother Church had been abandoned, new religions began to sprout up among the perverted. During the reign of Mary (1553-8) there was a brief reaction and Catholics had almost begun to look for the annihilation of the new creed. Her death, after a short reign of five years, was gladly welcomed by the Reformists. At this time John Calvin had been preaching his new doctrine in Paris and found many of the aristocracy in England ready to embrace his teachings. On the accession of Elizabeth to the throne of England she took severe measures to repel all this; and Catholics dissenting from the novelty of the reformation were punished by death at the stake, on the rack, by mechanical spears, and other devices too numerous to mention and too horrible to think of. In Ireland the state of affairs was even worse, religious houses were all suppressed and adherents to the Faith subjected to the most excruciating tortures. On the death of Elizabeth, James V1 of Scotland succeeded to the throne of England. The Irish Catholics had hoped for many favours on his accession, both as a descendant of Mary, Queen of Scots, a rigid Catholic, and also as having shown partiality to the religion in his youth. But in this they were to be disappointed, for James on all occasions enforced the laws enacted against them. When James died his son Charles succeeded him, but he was no better than his father.

Charles quarrelled with his own Parliament, who refused to give him money, and in order to procure it he promised many 'graces' to the Irish. But Lord Stafford, the King's Viceroy, hated the Irish and when they paid the money to the King he persuaded him to refuse the 'graces.' All Ireland was planted with English and Scotch Protestant settlers, and the King went on selling the land from which he drove the rightful owners away. All England was chaotic, and the Scots refused to take the religion Charles tried to enforce upon them, and a civil war broke out. The Parliament would not subsidize the King to fight Scotland, and he was obliged to make peace with them on any terms. When the Irish saw what Scotland had done, and how they now practised their own religion in peace, a great rising was planned. Owen Roe O'Neill was at that time a general in the Spanish army, and to him word of the Irish intention was sent. Meantime everything was arranged by the leaders, chief of whom was the famous Rory O'More. The great secret was kept up until the last night, when Dublin was warned, and the soldiers there marched upon the country. Most of the Irish leaders were seized, but Rory O'More escaped to France. The English troops were enraged at the outbreak of the Irish, and to revenge themselves, burned, laid waste and killed in every place they came to. It is said that for twelve miles around Dundalk neither man nor beast was to be found alive. But the most blood-thirsty leader of the Puritan army was Sir Charles Coote, then stationed at Trim. There is a copy of a pamphlet entitled 'A Collection of Some of the Massacres and Murders Committed on the Irish in Ireland Since the 23rd. October, 1641,' from which I take an account of the murders perpetrated in Meath under the directions of Sir Charles Coote.

'Mr. Barnwell, of Tobertinian, and Mr John Hussey, innocent persons, were hanged at Trim by Sir Charles Coote's party. Gerald Lynch of Dunover, aged eight years, was killed by troopers of Trim, in whose protection he was left. Mr. Thomas Talbot, of Crawleystown, about eighty years old, being protected, and a known servitor of the crown, was killed at his own door. About the Month of April the soldiers killed, in and about Navan, eighty men, women and children, who lived under protection. In April

1642, Mrs Ellinor Taaffe, of Tullaghanogue, sixty years old, and six women more were murdered by the soldiers of the garrison of Trim; and a blind woman aged eighty years was encompassed with straw by them, to which they set fire and burned her. The same day they hanged two women in Kilbride, and two decrepit old men that begged alms of then. In the same year Mr. Walter Dulin, an old man unable to stir abroad many years before the war, was killed in his own house, notwithstanding, that he was supposed to be under protection. Mr. Walter Evars, a justice of the peace and quorum, an aged man and bedridden of palsy, was carried in a cart to Trim and there hanged. Many ploughmen were murdered at Philbertstown. Forty men, women, and children reaping their harvest near Dunshaughlin were killed by a troop of the said garrison; and on the same day forty persons more, most of them women and children, shunning the fury of that troop, were overtaken and slaughtered. One hundred and sixty persons were killed by these soldiers near Rathcore, whereof there was one aged couple blind for fifteen years before. Upwards of 100 men, women and children were murdered at Mulhussy, and one, Connor Breslen was struck with a knife in the throat and bled to death. Ellinor Cusack, a woman upwards of 100 years was tied about with lighted brands and so tortured to death in Clonmoghan. James Dowlan, Donagh Comyn, and several other labourers to the number of 160 were slaughtered in the harvest fields of Trim.

A woman under protection was put into the stock of a tuck-mill, and so tucked to death. Many thousands of the poor inhabitants of Meath "were destroyed in the fire," and the rest for the most part perished with famine.'

But Coote the bloodthirsty monster met his end by the hand of one of his own soldiers. While pursuing the rebels at Trim he was shot from behind whether by design or accident was never known. The body was brought to Dublin, and there interred with great solemnity; "floods of English tears accompanying him to the grave"[4]

---

[4] Borlase- *A History of the Irish Rebellion.*

"Floods of English tears!" said O'Connell, *"Floods of English tears!"* This one fact at least is certain— that a more hideous, a more horrible villain never existed. The French revolution — fertile in sanguinary monsters — produced nothing like him, who spared neither man, woman nor child; neither priest nor lay-man. Yet this most superlative of diabolical miscreants was embalmed with English tears! *"English tears*! How heartily they wept for the man who was perfect in one talent —that of shedding Irish blood. A dry eye at *"his"* funeral would indeed have been *"un-English"*

On the 18th. March 1643, the agents of the Catholic Confederation, Lord Gormanstown, Sir Robert Talbot, Sir Lucas Dillon, and John Walsh, Esq., presented to the King's Commissioners at Trim a remonstrance of grievances in the name of the Catholics of Ireland, which remonstrance was transmitted to the King. This remonstrance underwent severe examination in the Irish House of Commons (from which all Catholic members had been expelled), and was then dismissed without the least disproof or contradiction of any of the grievances complained of, and without any resolution to rescind even the least severe restriction of the penal code. I quote a few sentences from this remonstrance, to show how faithful the Catholics of Ireland were to their religion in face of every terror, and what rights they were deprived of as citizens of the world:

'The Catholics of the Kingdom, whom no reward could invite, no persecution enforce, to forsake that religion professed by them and their ancestors for thirteen hundred years or thereabouts, are, since the second year of the reign of Queen Elizabeth, made incapable of places of honour and trust in Church or Commonwealth; their nobles being contemptible, the gentry debarred from learning in universities or public schools within this Kingdom; their younger brothers put by all manner of employment in their native country, and necessitated to seek education and fortune abroad; misfortunes made incident to the said Catholics of Ireland only, of all the nations in Christendom. They therefore most humbly beseech that you will vouchsafe gracious answers to these, their humble and just complaints, to prevent the further effusion of blood and to preserve the Kingdom from desolation. No matter whereof complaint is made in this remonstrance, they will ever pray for your Majesty's long and prosperous reign over them.'

The King might have granted the request asked him, but he was now at war with his own Parliament, and only a King in name. A couple of years later he was beheaded, and Oliver Cromwell came to Ireland to complete the work of desolation begun by Henry V111.

Daniel O'Connell At Trim

On the 19th. March 1843, Daniel O'Connell held a repeal meeting at Trim where 20,000 attended. When we come to Tara we will review the repeal year, and the mighty movement which awakened new hopes and aspirations in the down-trodden people. After this meeting the Hierarchy of Ireland under the presidency of Dr. Cantwell, Bishop of Meath, gave O'Connell a banquet at Trim, and the tribute he paid to the bishop will be long remembered in the diocese of Meath. In proposing his health he said:

"It is my pleasing duty to propose a toast. You will all anticipate what that toast is, and you know this, that his presence necessarily restrains me from speaking of him as I could wish; and if he even were absent, my heart would so outrun my mind that in my affection for the individual, I would forget the high station of his personal, political, and pastoral merits. Gentlemen, I congratulate you on having such a Bishop; I congratulate Ireland on having such a Bishop; and though there are more than one of them present, yet the inestimable advantage of having each with us, is not one bit the less important on that account nay, it means the more, for they are the constellation genius that enlightens our hemisphere, and that guides us and invigorates us in our moral struggle for the greatest of all political advantages. And would not the Repeal feed the hungry, clothe the naked, and open the prison house? Would it not found the monastery and the hospital, and the house of refuge for the destitute? Yes; it would perform

all the evangelical works of mercy, and therefore, it is my lords, that you use them. But how could they be but attentive to their country through centuries of bleeding oppression. Behold foreigners confiscating our property, taking away the goods and chattels of the people, robbing, plundering, murdering, scouring over the face of the land. Do not tell me that Ireland is not a nation; she has a national Church; she is a complete nation in her Church, for it has ever remained perfect, and is so still. England has not been able to strike it down; the foreigner was not able to put down our Church; the Penal Laws have not contaminated it; tyranny has not trampled upon it, and if the Irish monarch reigned to this day, the Church of Ireland could not be more perfect in all parts, in its ornaments, in all its efficacy, in all its holiness and fidelity."

Certainly, Trim has a history, civil and religious; it is all that it has now, except the institutions mentioned in my other paper; and a monument to the Duke of Wellington in the corner of its wide fair green, where it would be anything but pleasant to be on a wet day in March with the wind from the south-west.

Bective Abbey

Bective

...Roofless, doorless
shrineless, monkless, tho' it be.

Bective has the distinction of being the first really Irish Cistercian Monastery, founded through the munificence of an Irish prince, built by Irish hands, and tenanted by Irish inmates. Many regard the Cistercian monasteries as alien institutions, and part and parcel of the system synonymous with the regime of English rule and English Interests in Ireland. It is true, of course, that some of the Cistercian houses in the South and East of Ireland were endowed by the Anglo-Normans, but outside the borders of the Pale there were several monasteries, such as Bective, whose builders, inmates, and traditions were Irish in the fullest extent. The Cistercian Order was established in Ireland about 30 years before the Norman invasion, during which about 12 monasteries were founded, but even after that time the Irish princes continued to make grants of land to the Order, and helped in every way the establishment of the industrious religions.

The advent of the Cistercians in Ireland, 1142, was due to St. Malachy, one of Ireland's greatest saints. Mellifont was the parent house of this Order in Ireland. It was inhabited by a community of monks, partly Irish and partly French, trained and educated by St. Bernard in the Monastery of Clairvaux, France. At the instance of St. Malachy this company of religious was sent to Ireland, and a monastery founded by them at Mellifont. Bective was the first offshoot of Mellifont, founded between the years 1146 and 1151 by Murchard O' Melaghlin, King of Meath. The ruins of Bective fill a more striking object in the landscape to-day than those of Mellifont; the walls of the former rise up huge and grey, and are conspicuous from afar, while of the latter nothing can be seen until you burst in upon it, and even then with the exception of the old entrance gate, the chapter house, and the *lavabo*, a few stumps of pillars three or four feet high preserved from further decay by black caps of cement.

As was the custom of the Cistercian order a Latin name was given to their new settlement, the title of this (Bective) being *de Beatitudine,* from which some say the modern name, Bective originated. But I would not dream of holding to that theory. Bective derives its name from 'Begteach,' the "Little Palace," and it is probable that it was to Bective the Royal palace was transferred in 564, and hence 'Begteach.' The plan of the Cistercian monasteries was one peculiar to the order; a large cruciform church extending from East to West, with a large open space to the South, surrounded on three sides by cloisters connected with which was the domestic side of the Monastery. The latter with the dormitories above is all that remains of the original edifice, as the military castle, the most prominent feature in this present view was an annex of later days. The church, after the suppression, was removed and its materials utilised for secular purposes, the whole building, being turned into a private residence.

When Murchard O' Melaghlin died, Henry 11 granted the Kingdom of Meath to Hugh de Lacy, who became a no less munificent benefactor to Bective than the former King. He also improved the building until it fulfilled the two-fold purpose of an abbey and a fortress. The early inhabitants of Bective were an industrious brotherhood. The method of their lives was one of severe discipline, of great activity and industry. 2 o'clock a.m., was the hour for rising. The Office of Matins and Lauds were then intoned, which occupied an hour. For the next two hours masses were celebrated by the priests. At 5 o'clock the monks again repaired to the choir where Prime was sung, after which they assembled in the chapter house where a portion of the Rule was read, with extracts from the Martyrology, or lives of the Saints. On the conclusion of this the Prior allotted to each of the brethren his labour of the day. This was chiefly labour in the fields, or visits of charity to the people of the neighbourhood. After two hours spent thus, the monks again returned to the church for the Office of Tierce. They dined at 11.30, and afterwards rested for an hour. Precisely at 12.30 they rose and chanted the Office of None, after which outdoor labour was resumed. The evening was given to study. For those who were engaged in teaching, special times were allotted for this purpose. In Winter the hour for retiring was 7 o'clock; in Summer 8 o'clock.

From the 14th. September to Easter only one meal of vegetables was allowed. Meat, except in case of sickness, was never permitted. The Cistercian houses, and Bective was no exception, had in every respect self-supporting and self-sufficient institutions. They produced everything they needed; food from their own fields, gardens and orchards; fish from their own rivers; wool for their habits from their own sheep, they spun, wove, and wrought it themselves. They had their own mills; they grew, ground and baked their own corn. They had their own fuel, from the woods or the bogs; their own oil for their lamps. Moreover, every Abbey had its own school for the younger brothers of the order. The neighbouring youths were also admitted to these schools. The monastery was a technical as well as a literary school; it was also an agricultural school. Indeed, Irish agriculture owes much to the Cistercians. It was even more than this, it was an almshouse, a dispensary, and an hotel. The monks were highly skilled in medical science, and the whole neighbourhood benefited by their advice in times of sickness. All these services were gratuitously rendered. It was a home for the traveller, where he might make a long sojourn for rest and prayer. At the doors of the hospice, the poor were always welcome. All the surplus food was distributed to them daily, and the monks would sooner give their own allowances to the poor than have them go away hungry from their doors. At the time of Bective the people of Meath were merely pastoral, and knew but little of the cultivation of crops, except cereals alone. The monks of Bective were the first teachers in the methods of reclaiming land, tilling the ground. The surrounding population had ample opportunities of gaining information in the system of husbandry from the monks, as the farms and granges granted by De Lacy to the Abbey extended over a large portion of Meath and Westmeath. They also taught the people how to build proper houses for their own accommodation and sheds for their cattle; how to produce food for themselves and their flocks during the Summer months and to store it for the Winter.

In the course of time the abbots of Bective became large land-holders and employed a vast number of labourers in Meath and Westmeath. Honours and dignities, spiritual and temporal, were conferred on them, many of them being raised to the ranks of mitred abbots, and made peers of Parliament. They took part in all the councils of the king in Ireland, and figured highly in the political movement of the time.

There is a curious incident connected with the story of Bective. You all know how De Lacy, when proceeding to erect a castle at Durrow, King's County, lost his life, and how his decapitated body was buried where he fell. Ten years later, when his son, Walter, succeeded to the estates and honours of his father, the monks of Bective in order to secure his friendship, had his father's body exhumed and buried in the walls of the abbey, the head, by agreement, having been sent to the Priory of St. Thomas-a-Becket, at Dublin. De Lacy's wish was to be buried in the latter monastery. The Canons of St. Victor to whom the Priory of Thomas-a-Becket belonged, no sooner received the skull than they claimed the whole skeleton. For ten years a controversy was carried on between the two monasteries, which at length rose to such a pitch that the whole matter was referred to Rome. Pope Innocent 111 appointed a commission of enquiry to decide the question, and deputed De Rochefort, Bishop of Meath, and Gilbert, Prior of Duleek, as judges to decide the question between the claimants. The investigation resulted in favour of the Dublin Priory, so De Lacy's body was again taken up and finally buried in the Priory of Thomas street, Dublin.

When Richard, Duke of York, who was Governor of Ireland, unfurled his banner in the Wars of the Roses, the Monks of Bective, like all the gentry of Meath, leaned towards the Yorkist cause. And we afterwards hear that the Abbot supported the pretensions of Lambert Simnel in the first year of Henry the Seventh's reign. He was arrested, but afterwards pardoned, having sworn allegiance to the King. After this the abbey only figures faintly in the records of the time.

When Henry V111, commenced plundering the Church and confiscating the patrimony of the poor, Bective and all its broad acres in Meath and Westmeath was amongst the first to be spoiled. On the 31st. July the Abbot was forced to surrender. In 1552, during the reign of Edward V1, the possessions of Bective were sold to Andrew Wyse, Vice-Treasurer. The following is an authentic copy of the memorandum:

'Grant to Andrew Wyse, Vice-Treasurer, in consideration of the sum of £1,380. 16s 7d, Irish, of the Monastery of Bective with the manor and lordship and all edifices, churches, belfry, cemetery, woods, gardens, meadows, pastures, mills, and fishing weirs in the County of Meath; the manor of Revaghe, in the County of Westmeath, with court leet and view of frank pledge, fairs, markets, tolls, and customs, wards, messuages, and escheats, advowsons, donations, patronage of churches, vicarages, rectories, and all things spiritual arising out of the lands of Bective, Scriboke, Claidaghe, Ballgill, alias Grange of Ballgill, Ballradaghe, Douloughe, alias Dielogh, Cloneycollen, alias the Grange of Cloneycollen, the two Balbrios, alias Grange of Balbroy, Monteton, near Trim, Balsune, in the County of Meath; Renaghan, alias Renaighe, in the County of Westmeath; the rectories or chapels of Bective and Cladaghe, with all their houses, edifices, churches, tithes, altarages, and oblations belonging to same; to hold for ever by Knight's service, viz: by the service of one Knight's fee, as scutage runs in Ireland. Rent, £4. 5s. 4d, Irish.'

On the death of Andrew Wyse this property passed into the hands of Sir Alexander Fitton, who had married his daughter, Mary. Their daughter, Catherine, was married to Sir Robert Dillon, of Riverston. From the Dillons, Bective passed to Sir Richard Bolton, Lord High chancellor of Ireland, in whose family it still remains. Sir Robert Dillon had the Abbey converted into a dwelling house, traces of which may yet be seen. The ruins of the Abbey, thanks to the care of the Board of Works, are yet in a good state of preservation. But is it not a pity that the building had been altered from its original plan? Rather than remind one of a Cistercian

Monastery the ruins now standing present the appearance of a dilapidated mansion of the Elizabethan period. The upper story has suffered much by the change, and traces of mullioned windows and chimney shafts may yet be seen. In fact the whole church has disappeared, and what you now see towering above the Boyne is the massive remains of a Norman Keep.

Tara

> ' No more to chiefs and ladies bright
> The harp of Tara swells.'

Like the linden tree in Moore's beautiful poem, it is an instinct of man to turn homewards to his paternal soil, whether separated from it by seas of waters or oceans of time. And so I turn to Tara with the longing of a mariner outward-bound for his native shore, for Tara is my ancestral hone, now lost to me for ever, and soon to be forgotten as the residence of our fathers since we came with the Danes and learned to be more Irish than the Irish themselves. It may be for that reason that I always think on Omar Khayaam when I stand on Tara Hill and feel that the reviving herb that fledges the ramparts springs from the bones of my ancestors, who have resurrected again to a new life that will go on evolving until we have a more perfect man.— Away with all this! It looks atheistic, and I am not an atheist. But see the remains of that old mill, built on the site of the first corn mill ever erected in Ireland, by King Cormac to lighten the labours of his handmaid Carnaid, it used to be my father's when everybody had their own; and those broad acres and leopard-coloured woods, almost as far as Kilcairne, all these were ours one tine—but away with that thought also.

Tara, though not a high hill, commands a wide prospect of surprising beauty. On the North East the hill of Skryne rises with its lean tower swollen to the sky, hiding a wider view. The towers of Trim are plainly visible, and the white Boyne winding in and out through fields of waving green with here and there a hoary glimpse of some stately ruin that stands upon the lime-stone plain of Ireland, as landmarks of our history. The walls of Bective can be seen, and the smoking village of Kilmessan standing in a rich, but primitive wilderness of grass. Away to the South-East the blue hills of Wicklow notch the sky like a giant saw, and sometimes the smoke of Dublin rises in clouds, as if some huge censor was shaken to appease the wrath of an angry God. North-East on a clear day one can see the hills of Louth sometimes apparently shaking in the sunbeams as if some new Cuchulain was born and an earthquake like a great nurse was rocking him still.

To the North and North West the mountains of Cavan and Monaghan are clearly defined on a bright day, but always one can see the hill of Mullagh swollen up like the muscle of Ireland, and far South the heaving range of Slieve Bloom, nature's banner between the rival hosts Hy-Niall and Leagh Mogha. And under you, a little to the South-East is Dunsany Castle, the home of the Plunkett family to whom we are indebted for the most of our ancient monasteries. Thanks that the line has never run out, and still continues to run parallel across our history as noble and generous as of old. Lord Dunsany is a Plunkett, and a builder as you will find if ever you visit Dunsany. He has erected a beautiful recreation hall for the young men of the neighbourhood and keeps it well supplied with healthy literature, and several times in the year treats the school children to parties and concerts there. He has also built Bethmoora and Perdondaris, but Perdondaris fell and Bethmoora became desolate. Yet will they be remembered for ever. His lordship also preserves many tokens of his predecessors, and I had the privilege of wearing for a few moments, and holding in my sinful hands the Episcopal ring and Papal medals, and a watch of Oliver Plunkett the martyred Primate of Armagh.

All these things the recollection of Tara brings to mind, so that were we to treat everything it suggests in detail, it is a history, civil and religious of all Ireland I would be attempting. Let us review the existing remains of Tara and make a mental map of them so that when we come to talk of it we will know the sites of its many stories. You all know that formerly five great roads led to Tara, I will tell you about these roads afterwards, but for the present we will suppose that you come to Tara by the road from the South, succinctly called Slighe Dala, and still in existence. You turn to the left at the southern slope of the hill and first of all you meet the triple rampart of Rath Laoghaire. This was the private royal residence, and on the outer rampart the king is buried. (But we must sift this out, and probably we will find that Laoghaire is not buried at Tara at all). From Rath Laoghaire continue due north about eighty yards and we come to the outer rampart of Rath na Ree. But this was dug by idiotic vandals searching for the Ark of the Covenant, and can hardly now be traced.

Rath na Ree was also called Caihir Crofinn from the Tuatha de Danaan queen, who is very likely buried there. A little to the right, and within this enclosure, to the east, was Cormac's House—the scene of all his glories. It had a double rampart round it to divide it from the other buildings. Straight on across these ramparts was the Farradh, or Place of Meeting, where all the councils were held. Beyond this was the Mound of the Hostages, 'Dumha-na-Giall,' where the royal hostages were kept in chains of gold to indicate their value, but all the same they were strongly fettered lest they should escape. Beside this is the famous 'Lia Fail,' or Stone of Destiny. But oh horrors! I hear it has fallen and that the cattle are tramping on it. Let someone tell me this is not true.

Outside Rath-na-Ree was the well, 'Neamhnach,' still flowing away in a north-easterly direction. This was the site of the first corn mill in Ireland, built for the purpose of which I told you. Cormac got the idea of a water-mill during his foreign wars. Beyond Rath-na-Ree still was the Rath of the Synods, and north-east of this the Banqueting Hall. Just beyond this was the great 'Teach Miodhcuarta' or mid-court house. Its site can still be traced and must have been an immense structure. It was eight hundred feet long and eighty broad and had six great entrances to it on every side. We are told that the upper portion of this was for the accommodation of the warriors who came to the council of Kings, and the lower portion a kitchen for cooking for them, and it is said that some of the pots utilised on these occasions were capable of boiling several beeves and pigs.

But let us revert to the history of Tara, and I hope we will not lose our way down those miles and miles and miles of time, for we must retrace our steps back to the days when Abraham was offering sacrifices in the land of Canaan to come upon the first dun erected at Tara, nineteen hundred years before the Christian era. It is a long journey back to those tines, and yet according to the Four Masters, and I don't see why we should doubt them, Slainge, the King of the Firbolgs, chose Tara as his royal residence. It is however to the second colony that inhabited Ireland, i.e. the Tuatha de Danaan, that the origin of Tara is commonly traced. But it is a fact beyond all contradiction that Slainge was contemporary with Abraham, because when the Tuatha de Danaan came, Fal brought the stone of Destiny, which was the same upon which Jacob, the grandson of Abraham, rested and dreamed of the angels' ladder which fell from Heaven to Earth. So, if we are to trust legend and to believe, and I for one do, that Cathal, a Celtic King, brought this stone from Canaan to Spain, and entrusted it to the care of Fal, who brought it to Ireland at the invasion of the Tuatha de Danaan, and that these people found Ireland inhabited by the Fir-bolgs, i.e., Men of the Hills, there is no reason why we should doubt that Slainge reigned at Tara contemporaneously with Abraham. But this brings us to the Lia Fail.

There is great controversy about this magic stone; some holding that the large stone planted above the Croppies grave is the original stone of Fal, others arguing that it is the stone in the Coronation chair at Westminster Abbey. I hold with the former theory, as there is no record anywhere of the stone ever having been transferred from Tara, nor is it likely that the people would allow such a treasure to leave the country. The Lia Fail was the stone on which the Irish Kings were inaugurated, and it is said that were the King about to be elected not of true royal blood the stone would cry out against him, otherwise it was dumb. The legend says it was brought to Scotland by Fergus Mor Mac Earca that he might be inaugurated on it, and from thence it is said to have been taken, in the time of Edward 1, to Westminster. This is absolutely untrue, and the Lia Fail, the identical stone upon which Jacob slept, is yet at Tara, and readers, if you love the story of your country, don't allow this treasure to be reviled; it is bad enough to see it erect, serving the purpose of a scratching-post for cattle; but don't allow it to be trampled on by the brute beast—it would be a disgrace; it would be a sacrilege!

The Firbolgs Kings only reigned for a period of thirty seven years, and it is hardly probable that in such a short space of time they could have done much for Tara. The Tuatha de Danaan were a more civilised and a more powerful people. It is to them the Ogham writing is attributed. This race improved the royal residence of Tara, and must have been the first to erect stone buildings thereon. Kineth O'Hartigan, poet of the tenth century, calls Tara the cathair or city, so we may conclude that the stone buildings were then in vogue, and may accept the term of Tara, the capital city.

The ancient name of Tara was Cathir Crofinn, or the City of Crofinn, called after Crofinn, a Queen of the Tuatha de Danaans, remarkable for her beauty and her talents. Beyond all doubt she was buried in the rath that now bears her name. It is from the Milesian princess, Tea that Tara came by its name. The story goes on to say that when the Milesians saw Ireland in their dreams and set sail for it, Heremon, who was a King of that people, came with the first contingent and brought with him his beautiful queen, Tea. She, the queen, asked a favour of her lord while yet they were on the ocean, and it was, that he grant her the most beautiful hill in Ireland that she might be interred therein, and where every prince of her race might reign for ever. This favour was promised her, and on landing she chose 'Leath Drum,' the Beautiful Hill, which from her is called Tea Muir, i.e., Tara, the Mound of Tea. The Irish form of this word is 'Teamur,' Latinized, 'Temora,' which by a kind of metathesis has become Tara In the genitive case. Tea was buried at Tara as was her wish and some say, and it is very likely, that the Lia Fail was placed over her grave, and that its removal to its present site is quite modern.

Others hold that the stone was never removed from its original site, but that the Croppies were buried within its shadow. But coming to the Milesians so quickly we have skipped an elapse of several thousand years, and in order to give an idea of the religious practices of the Tuatha de Danaan, and their conflicts civil and religious with the Fomors, the 'dwellers of the water,' it is necessary to pick careful steps back to those mythical regions of time.

The people called the Tuatha de Danaan were a divine family

clustered round the goddess Danu; in this family we find the gods of light, wisdom, fertility and good. Of the Formors, ancient writings tell us they were demons of night, darkness, death, bane-ness and evil, the very antithesis of the Tuatha de Danaan. The Formors owed allegiance to a female divinity called Domnu; their King Indech is described as her son, and they are all called 'Domnus gods.' The word 'Domnu' signifies 'deep sea,' but these gods were afterwards called Formors, which is derived from two Celtic words which mean 'under sea.'

The Fomors were held to be more ancient than the gods, before whom, however they eventually fell. They were huge and deformed, some of them having but one arm or one leg, while others had the heads of goats, horses, or bulls. The most famous of these was Balor, whose father is said to have had the face of a cow. His name was Buarainech, that is 'the cow faced.' This monster Balor, seems to have combined in himself the qualities of a Cyclops and Medusa, the famous Gorgon of Grecian mythology. Though he had two eyes, one was always kept shut, for it was so venomous that however saw it immediately fell. The quality with which this eye was endowed was the result of an accident. Prompted by curiosity, he once peeped in a window where his father's sorcerers were preparing a magic potion, and the smoke from the boiling liquid reached his eye, imparting to it a deadly nature. Not even the gods could escape death from Balor's look, and he was only allowed to live among his own kindred on the condition that he kept his terrible eye closed. He was the greatest enemy of the Tuatha de Danaan, for when the tribes went to war, Balor was placed in the fore, and some of his own people from behind lifted up the eye with a hook and the unfortunate army upon which its gaze fell withered away. The 'evil look' is yet called in many parts 'Balor's eye.'

You will judge what struggles for existence the Tuatha de Danaan had during the lifetime of this monster. It was only after his death, or extermination, that the gods of Danu found peace in the land. I do not know what term to give the religious practices of these people; we know them as gods, and their stories tell us that their own influences brought about whatever changes was desired; and that the power of the Formors was for evil, while that of the Tuatha de Danaan was for good. It is however, very probable that the Tuatha de Danaan offered sacrifices, since they came from eastern countries where these practices were in vogue, and I am certain the hollowed ground of Newgrange tumulus was a receptacle for blood. As I have said, the Tuatha de Danaan were a powerful people and an intelligent people, and to them we owe the Ogham characters. Ogma is credited with having been the inventor of this alphabet It was originally intended for inscriptions on upright pillar posts, the equivalent for letters being notches cut across the face of the angle, the alphabet running as follows:-

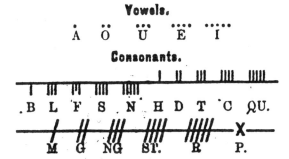

It was afterwards improved so that it could be written in manuscript, and instead of by dot the vowels were represented by short strokes through a horozontial line, thus:

As an illustration I will write "Slane," a short word in Ogam and English in order that you may have an idea of what ancient manuscripts must have been like:—

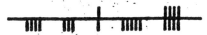

(Original newsprint from the Drogheda Independent - editor)

One hundred and twenty Kings of the Milesian race reigned at Tara from Heremon to the date of its cursing in 564AD. The history of that space of time would be that of all Ireland; and, as I told you before, my object is but to refer to the most noteworthy events in the annals specially connected with the Boyne and the place itself. Ollamh Fodhla was the fortieth on the list of these Kings; he died at Tara after a reign of forty years. His right name was Eochy; the term Ollamh Fodhla was given him as an agnomen on account of his wisdom and great learning. It was this King who instituted the 'Feis' at Tara, to which so many references are made in our ancient literature, sacred and profane.

Strictly speaking, this 'Feis' was the National Parliament of the Celtic tribes in Ireland, and exercised a great influence on the national life. It was held every third year for six days at Samhaintide, that is three days before and three days after November day. Its original object was to bring the tribes together, so that matters of national importance might be discussed, old feuds settled, and for the enactment of new laws, the assessment of tribute, the examination of the annals, and the maintenance of a militia to preserve law and order. During its session it was forbidden to wear deadly weapons, and any dispute between individuals or factions was punished by death. The place of every chief or representative of a clan was fixed with great exactness by the public heralds, their weapons having been taken from them and hung above their seats. When the day's work was over, feasting was begun, and prolonged to a late hour. During these pleasant interims, the bards of the tribes sang the songs of their heroes, and were rewarded with gifts varying according to the order of their merits. Or if the national affairs were disposed of before the lapse of the six days, the remainder of the time was given to sports; but martial exercises were forbidden lest they might lead to strife among the champions. But (I say this on my own authority) should a full moon happen while this council was seated, no sports were allowed, but all surplus time was devoted to the worship of their Gods. At such a time the Druids would come from their chambers with their scrolls and swords of gold to cut the mistletoe, and chant loud praises to the moon, and issue a proclamation that the next three days were to be held in silent veneration.

During the reign of Tuathal Teachtman, the triennial 'Feis' was exclusively for the purpose of discussing national affairs, and lost much of its former novelty. But in order to set a time apart for sport, this King directed that yearly assemblies be held in other parts of his dominions, ordaining that at Athboy a religious festival held at May; a great fair at Usnagh in mid-summer; and a marriage market, with games and sports at Telltown in August. But this was after he had widened his individual dominions by taking a portion from each of the old provinces to form a mensual Kingdom for the High-king.

Tuathal Teachtmar also required that the chiefs and kings assembled at the Feis-Tara should swear a solemn oath that they would bear allegiance to him, and be loyal to his house, and never set up against it a rival monarch. These were all wise regulations which tended to concentrate and consolidate the royal authority over the nation in one royal family. Alas, that so wise a King should be a party to an institution which caused much bloodshed at Tara, and red strife over the whole of Ireland for centuries. This was the establishment of the Borrumean Tribute. It happened in this way:

Tuathal had two beautiful daughters who were the delight of his life. (I, who am a dreamer never at home in the present, saw them first seated at the throne of their father singing strange songs. Their wide eyes were dark as sloes are dark in a thorn of shivering snow, and their hair was like moonlight in a wood). The King of Leinster sought the eldest in marriage and obtained his request; but no sooner had he brought her home to his dun at Naas, than he heard the younger was the more beautiful. So after a short time he sent a false message to Tuathal saying that the princess had died, and that he now sought the hand of the younger sister.

Tuathal granted this request also, and the princess was sent to him. But no sooner had the sisters met, than the eldest of them died of shame at the deceit practised against herself and her sister, and the younger shortly afterwards died of grief at the fate of her sister.

The truth of the whole matter reached the ears of their father, and the Kings of Ulster and Connaught, who were their foster-fathers, and immediately a great army was raised. Leinster was harried with fire and sword; the wicked King was slain, and the princes and people of Leinster were forced to pay annually a tax of 1,500 sheep, 1,500 pigs, 1,500 kine, several querns, and a brazen boiler large enough to hold twelve oxen and twelve pigs. For five hundred years this tax was the cause of continuous bloodshed. It was never levied without a fight, and often was successfully resisted. It was the cause of hatred, strife and slaughter between the kingdoms until its final remission through the prayers of St. Moling.

But it produced a lasting effect of a great estrangement between the men of Leinster and Conn's people, which resulted in the fact that the Lagenians took sides with the Danes at Clontarf; and at a later date its influence moved false Diarmaid Mac Murrogh to bring in the Normans in order to be revenged on his own countrymen.

Cormac Mac Art is the next conspicuous figure on Tara, and the most. Tara never saw his like before, and never will again He is the hero of Tara's romance, and the champion of its prerogatives. Behold him, according to Kineth O'Hartigan, seated at the head of the princes of Erin. He is wrapped in a mantle of crimson, that is fastened at his breast with a brooch of gold. A golden belt girdles his loins, and sandals of purple are on his feet. He has made Tara as your mind's eye sees it now, a sunny city of feasts, a world of perishable beauty. The monuments of Tara were his creations and glory; he was himself a candelabra in the midst of all its galaxy. No, Tara never knew a King before him so worthy of its crown, nor after, nor ever again. And he was more than a King; he was a scholar, a sage, and a law-giver. Even his works yet are with us; at least in outline, challenging our administration. He it was who assembled the chroniclers of Ireland at Tara, and ordered them to unite what history they had written in one book, called the 'Psalter of Tara.' It is a lost work now, but tradition tells us that it contained the history of Ireland from Noah's Flood.

Of the great compilation known as 'Senchus Mor,' Cormac may be regarded as the author; at least he laid the foundations for it. It is in this book we find Cormac as a law-giver. The work known as 'Teagasc na Riogh' is attributed to Cormac, and is said to have been written by him for his son's (Cairbre) instruction when he himself was unable to reign, having lost an eye in battle. As a warrior, Cormac is equally renowned. He engaged In fifty battles against his foes, north, south, east, and west. He was the patron of Finn Mac Cool and his warrior band known as the 'Fianna of Erin,' and these really composed his staff. In appreciation of Finn's wisdom and valour he gave him his daughter Grainne to wed. The princess however, eloped with Diarmaid. Their wanderings through Erin are the theme of many a song.

Cormac was also a great builder. He erected a rath which bears his name at Tara, and enlarged the banquet hall. He built the first water-mill ever erected in Ireland in order to lessen the labour of his servant Carnaid. When he came to die, he charged his people not to bury him at Brugh with the pagan Kings, although he himself was a pagan. He requested to be buried at Rossnaree facing the dawn. His followers, deeming this to be his death-ravings, essayed to bring his body across the Boyne for interment with his pagan sires. But each attempt was futile as the river drifted them back to the Rossnaree bank at every attempt. His remains were finally deposited at Rossnaree to wait the call of Michael, when Time is rolled up like a scroll, and heaven and earth are blotted away.

The next memorable event on Tara is the coming of Patrick and the battles of the old religion and the new. Before I pass on to this, I will tell you what I know about Druidism, the religion of Nature, as practised by our fathers before the advent of Christianity. The priests of this religion were called Druids, a word derived from the Aryan speech, D.R., meaning a tree.

Druidism.

'Their mystic creed was woven round
The changeful year— for every hour
A spirit and a sense they found
A cause of piety and power.

The crystal wells were spirit springs,
The mountain lakes were peopled under,
And in the grass the fairy rings
Exceeded rustic awe and wonder.

Far down beneath the western sea
Their paradise of youth was laid,
In every oak and hazel tree
They saw a fair immortal maid.'

The Druids were held in high estimation, ranking second only to the kings and chiefs. They were the priests, the scientists, the wizards and historians of the people, all spiritual power, and all human knowledge was vested in them. They were exempt from all contribution to the State, and any offence against them was punishable by death. Their decisions in spiritual matters were final and those who disobeyed them were laid under a bann and boycotted. They never allowed their doctrines to be put in writing, and so very little of their teaching is known. When Julius Caesar landed in England he investigated Druidism and wrote all the facts he collected in a book called *De Bello Gallico.* From this book we learn that Druidism taught the transmigration of souls. This doctrine was inculcated in the people, and encouraged the warriors to deeds of valour through disregarding the fear of death. (We read that Finn Mac Cool was re-born after his death, as a king in Ulster, named Morgan.) This idea, however, belonged to the metaphysical side of Druidism, and was not as important to the primitive mind as ritual and sacrifice, by which the gods were appeased. Among the Druids this humouring of the gods took the shape of human sacrifices. Those who were afflicted with disease or engaged in warfare either sacrificed human beings for victims or Immolated themselves. The Druids were employed as ministers for such sacrifices, for it was their teaching that unless the life of man be repaid by the life of man, the will of the gods could not be appeased. They also ordained that national offerings should occasionally be paid, and on such an occasion the victim was wound in wicker, which was set on fire. In Ireland the national offering was held at Ballymagauran in County Cavan. From this the place received the name of Mag Slecht, the 'Plain of Adoration.' It was here 'Crom Cruagh' the great idol which fell on St. Patrick's approach was raised.

> 'To him without glory
> They would kill their piteous, wretched off-spring
> with much wailing and peril,
> To pour their blood around Crom Cruagh'
> (Dr. Kuno Meyer)

But Druidism had also its poetical side. They imagined the sky, moon, the earth and the sea, the mountains, streams, and woods to be ruled by beings like their own Kings. Every passion and craft, such as poetry, love, war and smithcraft had its divine founder, and exponent, and persons excelling in art were entrusted to the care of a special divinity. The oak tree was specially revered, as being the foster father of the mistletoe which was related to the sun and moon. At every full moon the mistletoe was cut with a sword of gold and prayers and hymns sung to it for the three following days.

Two religious festivals were held every year in honour of the sun, in June and in December. For as the heat of Summer increased a fear would seize the people that the earth would be burned, and they offered prayers to it in the woods, and believed that the decrease of heat on Autumn approach was brought about by their supplications. In December they feared that the sun was leaving them altogether and held a festival in its honour, entreating it to come back with heat and flowers and singing birds. They had special reverence for wells, and in certain parts of the country days were given to water feasts. On these occasions the people of the neighbourhood all met together at a well-side and after praying with the Druids enjoyed themselves in sports and pastimes, and in the evening carried to their homes water from the well, which being specially blessed on that day, was held to be an unfailing therapeutic to all sickness until that day year.

iii

St. Patrick At Tara

'Be still: the skies are choked with thunder,
lightning, and fierce wind,
For God has heard and speaks His angry mind;
Go cast your bodies on the stones and pray,
For He has wrought midnight and dawn and day.'
-W. B. Yeats

Between the Rath of the Synods and the great Banqueting Hall, the five great roads that led to Tara had their meeting point. It is said that these roads were made by the fairies on the night Conn was born. In all probability it was on that night they were opened, Cormac deferring the occasion until that event. These roads can yet be faintly traced, stretching for the most part in the direction of the present trunk railway lines. Standing at the meeting point of these roads on the eve of Easter A.D. 433, one of the King's (Laoghaire) Druids beheld a huge red fire on Slane Hill.

Now a great feast was about to be held at Tara, and it was forbidden to light any fire in Ireland before the Druid fire of Tara. St. Patrick, being apprised of this at Slane, thought it an opportune moment in which to bring himself into prominence in the land, anticipating that his transgression of the law would bring him into the presence of the High King. There was much confusion at Tara when the Druid announced the fire on Slane hill, and at the same time made a prophecy that it would never be extinguished. A strong band was immediately dispatched for Patrick, and in the early morning himself and his few followers arrived at Tara as prisoners of the King.

Laoghaire was struck by the calm and holy countenance of the saint, and had him released from chains, to the consternation of the vast assembly which had collected in fear and curiosity. A Druid offered him a cup of ale which he had previously poisoned, but Patrick blessed the cup, and tilting it a little the poison flowed out. The Druids then challenged him to work wonders, and on Patrick accepting the challenge the Druid caused a fall of snow. Patrick challenged him to remove it, but in this he failed, as his power was only for evil, but the Saint blessed it and it immediately disappeared. The Druid then brought a thick darkness over the land, but Patrick blessed the darkness, and the sun shone as before. Laoghaire then interposed, commanding that each should throw his book into the stream, and the one which came out uninjured should belong to him who had the true God. But the Druid objected to this, and said the water was Patrick's God, then the King said *"Cast them into the fire,"* but again the Druid objected on the ground that the fire was also the God of the Saint. Patrick settled the matter by proposing that two houses be built, and that the Druid with his (Patrick's) chausible should go into one, and a follower of his, with the Druid's cloak around him, into the other, both houses, then, to be set on fire. This was agreed to, and accordingly done. A mighty marvel was seen when both houses were reduced to ashes. The Druid who wore the saint's chausible was burnt to a cinder, while the garment remained unsinged, and the cloak of the Druid was burned from the shoulders of St. Patrick's follower, while the youth himself was uninjured.

The King was enraged at this, and would have slain Patrick, but God scattered his men, and slew thousands of them that day. The wicked King became frightened at this, and kneeling down, was baptised by Patrick, but he only believed with a half a heart and died a pagan. That is the reason why I am doubtful about Rath

Laoghaire, and not certain if the King is buried there. It is very likely the Christians did with him what they did to another King in Ulster who did not accept the Faith, lifted him by night and buried him face downwards in a bog. The story of Patrick at Tara is so well known that it is useless my going any further. You know how he illustrated the mystery of the Blessed Trinity with the shamrock. But the spirit of Druidism lurked at Tara long after Patrick's death. Oilioll Molt, the immediate successor of Laoghaire, was a pagan, and died the pagan's death, so did *his* successor, Laoghaire's son, Luaghid. Druidism was not finally abolished until 564AD, when another memorable scene occurred on Tara Hill: this was The Cursing of Tara.

The Cursing of Tara

The High King at this time was Diarmaid, son of Fergus Cearbhoil, a noble prince and an accomplished one, who was resolved to maintain peace and order throughout the land. But alas, that in his good purpose he should be ultra strict, and acted in a high-handed manner that brought him into conflict with the saints of the land.

There is abundance of evidence to show that Diarmaid kept Druids in his court and was secretly attached to the Druidical rites, but against that again he was generous to Clonmacnoise and did much for the furtherance of Christianity. But his high-handedness brought him into conflict with St. Columcille, his own cousin whom he insulted at Tara by tearing from-the saint's arms a homicide who had unconsciously slain one of the King's soldiers. This outrage raised Ulster to arms against him and was the cause of the battle of Cuildreimnhe where he was defeated; but even this was not warning enough for him. Calling a meeting of his stewards and heralds, he ordered them to march through the country and see that the King's peace was preserved, and to carry their spears crosswise, and whatever doorway was not wide open to admit their passing through to hew it down.

In this manner they came upon the dun of a chief in the southern extremity of what is now County Galway. This chief was about to be married, and had some time previously renovated his dun, and raised a palisade of oaken posts over the earth work. When the steward of the High King came to this place, he was unable to carry his spear crosswise through the entrance, so he attempted to hew down the door. On seeing this the chief drew his sword and with one stroke cut his head off. This was treason against the King and the chief knew it, so he fled for refuge to St. Ruadhan of Lorragh. But Ruadhan also feared the King, and advised the chief to fly to the King of Wales for safety. This, he accordingly did, but even there the King demanded his extradition, so in despair once more he sought refuge from Ruadhan. A whisper reached the King that the chief was in hiding at Lorragh, so that he came in person to seek him. On hearing this the saint and the chief together dug a deep hole in the floor of Ruadhan's cabin, and hid Guaire there. The King and his soldiers searched the house of the saint and failing to discover the ill-fated chief were about to return when a happy (?) idea struck the King. Knowing the saint would not tell a lie, he turned to him and said, *"Where is Guaire?"* Whereupon the saint replied, *"I know not where he is if he is not in this house."* Another search was ordered and the unhappy chief was discovered and immediately carried off to Tara.

Now this was a violation of the right of sanctuary; so Ruadhan summoning the aid of the two Saint Brendans and many other saints whom he had known at Clonard, proceeded to Tara and demanded the chief. The King refused their request, but they were not to be put off. They fasted for a year against the King and plied him with miracles, but Diarmaid gave them back prodigy for prodigy. (It would seem from this that once more there was a conflict between the saints and the Druids). Day and night the saints uttered condemnation against Diarmaid with candles and bells. Several of the Royal youths began now to die without any apparent cause. The King, too, had a dream in which he saw a large tree spreading on Tara Hill and strangers hewing it down. *"I am that tree,"* he said, *"and the strangers who hew me down are the clergy."* So when he rose he yielded to the saints and gave up the chief. At the same time addressing Ruadhan he said, *"I'll have ye done to undo my Kingdom, for I maintained the righteous cause. And, Ruadhan, may your diocese be the first to be ruined in Ireland, and may your monks forsake you!"* And so it came to pass.

Then upon the royal hearth Ruadhan imprecated utter ruin— *"That never more should smoke issue from its roof-tree."* The King died a violent death the following year, and no king after him, although they were called the kings of Tara, ever dwelt there. It is very probable, as I have said before, that the royal residence was removed to Bective after this.

Tara was later chosen by St. Adamnan as a place to hold great ecclesiastical synods. It may be that this saint sought to prepare Tara once more for the seat of the monarchy, for we hear that a great synod of the chief and prelates of Ireland was held there in 697AD, and prayers offered up for the uplifting of Ruadhan's curse. What a pity it is that the home of hundred kings should be thus cursed desolate; that the lowing of cattle should now be heard where once the voice of the bard wandered round in song; that grass should grow in its empty courts, and no more forever be heard the revels of its warriors and its sages! What have we done against Heaven at all that we should be so accursed? Nothing! We only sinned against ourselves. Pride, Pride. PRIDE!—loud thing of baubles and of gaudy dress and emptiness will you never let us be? Will you never cease from luring us, as the Sirens lured Ulysses when wandering home from the plains of Troy. Is this your work? No need to answer; it is written on the forehead of the country.

Cast your eyes around the ranches of Meath, and see Pride in her poverty. The sighing of the unlaboured fields are pronouncing a severe judgement on the air; ay, are sending our able-bodied across the sea in dozens, and to the lunatic asylums in scores. We are the greatest idlers in the world, we Meathians. But we must shortly mend our ways or leave the country, as the dawn of an era in labour is in the sky. We must be prepared to strip off our collars and ties and wear frieze once more, and make a friend of the spade instead of the broken down aristocrat, or else the rising generation will evacuate us. We must till our fields instead of letting them to the man of cattle, and we must not think our sons and daughters too grand for a trade.

iv

"The Nation have fallen, and thou art still young,
Thy sun is but rising, when others are set;
And tho' -slavery's cloud o'er thy morning hath hung,
The full moon of Freedom shall beam round thee yet."

—Moore

Never through all her dark centuries of oppression has Ireland lost hope. The Niobe of Nations though she has been; weeping for her beloved fallen and the rights of God wrested from her hands by the tyrannical usurper, through her tears she has seen the rainbow of hope bending from the clouds of her sorrow like a splendid promise of sun, and she stood up with her cross, hopeful and beautiful and strong. It is easy for us now, who breathe on the verge of Freedom[5] and have full liberty to air our political and religious feelings, to hold out our hands and say *"Tomorrow it comes"* and *"Tomorrow,"* but when we look back to our fathers of the Penal Days or sweep with the eye of our mind the bloody fields of '98, or the homes of our people during the artificial famine, we wonder how hope survived in the breasts of our people, or gathered strength to swing a far lamp on the horizon of brighter times.

And more especially in the Penal days when the broken Treaty of Limerick hung like a millstone from the necks of the people and

---

[5] Anticipation of the enactment of Home Rule.

no chief remained to them to bid them cast off this yoke and make another stand for freedom; although they had been dying for the liberty of other countries away beyond the seas, had been marshals of other armies, counts, barons, and knights of other lands, and prime ministers of other senates. And when the Penal Laws had been abolished and Grattan's Parliament inaugurated, the country was once more disappointed in their hopes for brighter days. Not but that this Parliament might have done much to alleviate the woes of the people were it allowed to reform itself; but all Catholics were shut out from it, and a great many of its members held government offices or received pensions from the English, and these were always in opposition to Grattan's party, and opposed their every plan.

Secret societies began to spring up all over the country composed of Protestants and Catholics, and now and then these broke out in little local brawls, and often committed most dastardly outrages. Then Wolfe Tone, a Protestant lawyer, determined to organise a great society in which all Irishmen of every creed and clan should join for the good of their country. This was called The Society of United Irishmen; thousands became members, avowed enemies of England, determined to break away from English rule as Americans had done; but the Government were on the watch and paid a number of spies to join the organisation and betray the plans of its leaders. Pitt, a just and wise minister of the Parliament of England, determined to bring back peace to Ireland by what is called Catholic Emancipation: that is, the granting to Catholics the same freedom as their Protestant neighbours. Lord Fitzwilliam came to carry out this scheme and was received in Dublin with great joy. But George 111 had a dread of Catholics and could not be made to believe they were worthy of being trusted, so he summoned Lord Fitzwilliam back to England again. Naturally this disappointment of their hopes filled the people with anger and bitterness. The United Irishmen now became a secret society and plotted a rebellion, availing themselves of the opportune moment when England was at war with France. Wolfe Tone sailed to France for help, but it was little they could spare Ireland in their own crux. Through his cleverness, although he could not even speak French, he persuaded members of the French Government to attack English power in Ireland, offering them the help of the United Irishmen. An expedition of 43 ships with 15,000 troops set sail for Ireland, but a great storm arose in mid ocean and only 19 landed. These waited for the rest of the fleet, but at last in despair cut their cables and sailed for France again. But the English were warned and through their spies they learned that Lord Edward Fitzgerald had taken over command of the United Irishmen. He was arrested in Dublin and died of the wounds he received attempting to escape. And now the yeomen were let loose upon the country to flog, hang, and torture the peasants whom they suspected of being rebels, burning cabins, levelling homes and laying the land waste. Father Murphy rose against them in Wexford, and for a long time held out against them, but when Vinegar Hill was taken his band dispersed, broken and hopeless.

Many of these came as far as Tara and there made another stand, but overpowered by numbers they were slaughtered like sheep by the yeomen, and shovelled into one large grave in the shadow of the Lia Fail, where they sleep the long sleep of Death assured of their resurrection. God give them eternal rest!

Still this Rachel of the North had a hope for her children, though now her freedom was sold and she was yoked to England by the chains of the Union. And now emigration began in earnest. Year by year the hearts blood of Ireland leaked away from her breast, to swell the veins and accelerate the pulse of progress in strange and far off lands. The trade and commerce of the country was neglected or made impossible, the fields became bare wilderness, the mills dumb. The broad heel of coercion was on the heart of the country crushing the very life of her. Heavy taxes burgled her industry; increased rent laid her fields wild, and many a happy home desolate. Gasping, she lay, this beautiful mother of brave ones, hoping on, and on, and on, while all her echoes took the wailing of her beloved round the bare and wind-swept hills from the hearths about to be vacated, and the sounds of the Battering Ram.

All this she silently endured for years, as if it was her welcome deserts, until there rose up in the midst of her people a Messiah who lit the fire of agitation in every one of her homes, and, as John Boyle O'Reilly said *"fanned it with his breath."* This was Daniel O'Connell, who in the year of Ireland's sufferings, 1843, hoisted the banner of Repeal for the purpose of completing the emancipation of the Irish people. He inoculated the people with fire; hammering it home to their spirits that there was but one hope — that the only panacea for the National grievances, the only means by which the industries of the country could be restored, was in Home Rule, self legislation, the repeal of the Act of Union. The movement began, and flooded the down-trodden people with new hopes, and new spirit. It fell like a match on a prairie and fired the country with a new determination. Monster meetings were held everywhere; and in a short time the whole Irish nation joined hands in the new movement. The exiles abroad looked back to the old land of their affection, visualizing happy days for their kindred at home, and a speedy return to the home of their childhood. The people expected that the colossal movement would permeate with national feelings the Irish members of the British Parliament, and induce them to legislate in an Irish spirit for the Repeal of the so-called Union, that only brought misery and desolation to their country. One of these monster meetings was held in Longford on the 25th. May; another in Tullamore, Kings County, in July; but these and the hundred others fall into insignificance when compared with the great National Convention on the Hill of Tara on the memorable 15th. August 1843. Several historians alleged that this was the greatest political meeting ever held in any country. And it is something to boast of, when our morality is challenged, that in a gathering of **one million five hundred thousand**, not one act of intemperance, not one angry word, was committed. One million five hundred thousand, I could hardly put it down in figures, attended this great convention. No wonder the great Liberator, carried away by enthusiasm, shouted out in a loud voice on beholding the assembly:-

"0! Good Heavens! What a multitude!"

All through the preceding night, thousands and tens of thousands from the north, south, east and west and from everywhere, north-east, southeast and from every point of the compass, poured through the towns and villages, playing national tunes on pipe and violin, while bands loud on some souls-stirring battle march of old were heard miles away. The neighbouring town and villages were unable to accommodate the massive contingents en route for Tara. But nothing daunted, they slept in dozens by the hedges, and in outhouses at the farms, while thousands proceeded to Tara in order to get a good position near the platform on the morrow.

Early on the next morning twenty masses were celebrated on the Hill, the priests exhorting the people to violate no law that day, but show themselves worthy of the liberty they came there to demand. When O'Connell was observed making his way up the Hill heads were un-bared and a loud cheer went up to greet him— loud enough to level the walls of 150 Jerichos, loud enough to show the oppressors of the people that they wanted to be free. One million five hundred thousand hands were raised palpitating with the fire of enthusiasm— hands ready at a moment's notice to wield the sword for the freedom of their country.

O'Connell ascended the platform, and in a voice of thunder asked the multitude if they demanded the Repeal of the Union. He, with elocution that has never been equalled for its pathos and determination, recalled to the memories of the vast populace her individual grievances, and many torments to which Ireland was subjected; he drew up a prophetic picture of Ireland under self-government and on the canvas of the people's minds outlined bright prospects, picturesque homes, and revived industries under self-government, at the same time exhorting the Irish members at present administering the cruel laws of England to a sense of God's justice, and reminding them of the obligations with which they were incumbent as representatives of the people now congregated together, to carry back to them their erstwhile peace, rejuvenate their old prospects, and revive the fallen industries.

He encouraged the people in the display of valour they had exhibited that day, and assured them that by their united efforts the cause which they came there to plead would be granted them in the near future. But though he spoke in a voice of thunder, there were thousands who were unable to get within a hearing distance, and those turned their attention to the Croppies grave, the resting place of the valorous youths who had sacrificed their lives for the freedom of which they were robbed. 'Dean' Cogan, who was present at this assembly, tells us that it would take a tear from a stone to witness the grief of the old men and women, who availing themselves of the opportunity, came to Tara to view the grave of their fathers, husbands and children who were cruelly sabred by the yeomen in the red year of '98. The scene around the graves of these brave men was truly impressive when the recollection of Ireland's past history was brought back to them while gazing around at the imposing ceremonies of that day. And not one of the vast multitude turned away from Tara without dropping a tear and a prayer for the young men and old who had given their lives for the cause of their country far away from their homes and all that was dear to them. The proceedings of the day terminated in a banquet to O'Connell at which upwards of a thousand gentlemen were present. The Chairman being Mr. Boylan, of Hilltown House, Bellewstown. The mighty movement which was inaugurated by O'Connell has never crumbled away. It is with us still as fair and as fresh of old; it was no splendid phantom which would fade away after the enthusiasm of the moment had subsided; it has been handed down to us as a heritage ever novel and ever new.

Watergate Street and Flower Hill

Navan

Navan is the ugliest and very best provincial town that I have ever stood in. There is nothing stagnant about it except the water in the street puddles. It is a town where business is ever on the move, alive to every modern improvement in agriculture, and the first to grasp any movements towards the advancement of the country's good. Though not in name, Navan is the county town of Meath. The Co. Council hold their offices there, and all the committees that watch over the rights of the people of Meath meet there, and every society whose object it is to further the interests of the community has its meeting place in Navan. It is peopled by men and women far noted for their industry. To this I would also add their hospitality, from which I get it so hard to tear myself away every time I go to Navan. I say Navan is an ugly town, and immediately regret it. It may be that I do not like its hilly square or the bad repair of the streets; but no man can stand on that square on a fine day in Spring looking up Flower Hill with its jumble of roofs, slate and thatch, blue and grey and yellow in bland confusion. And no man can view Navan from the 'Round 0,' with its heaps of gables and its blue smoke, and listen to its old song of labour, which has built up cities and mowed jungles, and say Navan is an ugly town.

I spent some of the most delightful days of my life at Navan, and would recommend anybody not acquainted with its environments to come to it in Spring, or at the fall of the leaf, and take a walk down the rampart as far as the horse bridge, and look back at the town. Such a muddle of beauty I never saw before. In the canal there is the coloured shadows of beautiful trees and Spicer's Mill, and in the Boyne a quaking glory of coppice and woods and roofs, and over all, in the spring-time, the loud thrush and the far blackbird make the very air tremble in their delightful passions.

Navan is very advantageously situated in regard to railway communication, and there is splendid waterway connection with the port of Drogheda. This, as we are all sorry for, has recently become derelict, but the Navan Urban Council and the Corporation of Drogheda have opened negotiations with the County Council with a view to re-opening it on new lines. Let us hope that some agreement may be arrived at before the Railway Co. snaps it up to close it ever as they have done with many another throughout Ireland.

Navan is 25 miles from Dublin, and is connected with the Metropolis by a double line of railways, to the Broadstone and Amien's St. The present town of Navan is quite modern when compared with Drogheda or Trim, as it was not built until after the Anglo-Norman invasion. The old town was made of wattles, and situate at Balreask, where until a few years ago there were the remains of a Church founded by St. Columb. When the present town was built, De Lacy, in consequence of its central position had it walled in, and divided its ancient principalities amongst his Knights, the town of Navan falling to a Knight named Nagle. Under this family Navan became a flourishing town, and was the first borough established in the palatinate of Meath. It received a Charter from Edward IV, and from Henry V11 additional privileges.

In 1539 the Northern Irish under Con O'Neill and Manus O'Donnell invaded the English Pale, and, amongst other Anglo-Irish towns, plundered Navan, carrying away with them gold and silver and many articles of value. To guard against any further raids of the Irish it was enacted by Henry V111 that every plough-land in Meath and Westmeath should be charged with a payment of 3s. 4d for four years, for the purpose of re-building the walls, and renovating the breaches made by the Irish. Additional privileges were granted to the citizens of Navan by James 1 and Charles 11. Navan sent two representatives to the Irish Parliament.

The ancient name of Navan was Nuacongbhail, called after an early convert of St. Patrick's, who built an abbey where the soldiers' barracks now stands. In this abbey there was an image of the Blessed Virgin under which many miracles were wrought. I will refer to this again. At the close of the twelfth century Joceline de Anguls rebuilt the abbey of Nuacongbhail for regular canons following the rule of St. Augustine. This abbey, on account of the miraculous image referred to, was dedicated to the Blessed Virgin, and since then the parish of Navan has continued under the same patronage. The last abbot of Navan was Thomas Wafre; and on July 19th, 1539, the Commissioners of Henry V111 summoned him to surrender. Assembling his community in the chapter house he laid the facts before them soliciting their advice. However they remonstrated that there was nothing for them to do but sign their own expulsion, agreeing as it were to the plunder of their monastery. The image of the Blessed Virgin held so long in veneration was now torn down from its pedestal and with many another sacred object of devotion was publicly burned on the Market Square.

And now the doors of the abbey were shut for ever and its monks dispersed, roofless and homeless orphans of the world. In the course of time the abbey was reconstructed and changed into a military barracks, I am proud to say that recently this building has been converted into dwelling houses for the poor of Navan. In the burial ground adjoining the old abbey there were the remains of many ancient tombs beautifully sculptured, but these have been torn and broken up to pave the barrack yard, and the cemetery has been converted into a garden. While these acts of vandalism were being enacted many skulls and bones were dug up and shovelled into the Blackwater; and it is related that about the close of the eighteenth century a Colonel named Bishop, who had command of the barracks, seeing a splendidly carved tombstone enquired who was the occupant within. On being told it was the grave of a bishop he immediately ordered that it be broken up swearing by his Creator that only one Bishop would rule there. —— He dropped dead shortly after.

On sinking the pump in the barrack yard in 1854, the remains of nine persons were discovered. In 1772, the chapel of Navan fell, and the people found themselves without a place of worship. For months and months the Holy Sacrifice of the Mass was offered up in a sentry box procured from the barracks. This was carried, on a

Sunday morning to the laneway at the corner of Mr. Sheridan's hardware shop and there the people knelt on the bare ground, while the priest officiated in the awkward shelter which this could provide. A mud wall barn, on the site of which the present chapel is built, was next procured. This barn was used during the week by farmers for threshing operations, and on Sunday evenings the little boys and girls of the town attended to sweep it out and decorate it for the following day. The altar was made up of planks, supported on barrels, but the flowers were of the fields and the lanes, and the poor, rude building formed a pretty picture. The Penal Statute against Catholic belfries was then severely enforced, but the parishioners of Navan hit on a pretty device which enabled them to escape this. They suspended a bell on the gable end of a brewery owned by a Catholic gentleman and this served the dual end of calling the men to work, and the people to pray.

But reverting to the miraculous image of Our Lady of Navan, I take the following story from Hardiman's *Statute of Kilkenny*:

'In the abbey church of Navan there was an image or statue of the Blessed Virgin held in great repute, to which persons from all parts of Ireland - princes and peasants, rich and poor-were in the habit of making pilgrimages. In the Parliament of Dublin, 1454, amongst other Acts it was ordered that letters patent of the King be made for taking into protection all people, whether rebels or others, who shall go in pilgrimage to the Blessed Virgin at Navan. In a Parliament held at Drogheda, A.D., 1460, Henry V1 under Richard Duke of York, an Act was passed summoning Thomas Bathe, Knight, pretending himself to be Lord of Louth to which he had no right of inheritance, to appear before the Prince on the Tuesday before the next St. Patrick's Day, under penalty of forfeiture of all his property, and of being excluded from the King's protection to answer the charges of which he was accused.

In the preamble of this act it is stated that Bathe, for the purpose of obtaining the King's favour suborned one of his servants to accuse Dr. John Stackboole on of the dignities of the Abbey of

Navan of high treason, for which he was imprisoned in Dublin Castle, sent to England and there vindicated and set free; that Bathe next robbed Dr. Stackboole and refused to make restitution; that Dr. Stackboole being in despair of any remedy against the extortion, violence and oppression of the said Bathe, wrote to the Pope and obtained an order for Dr. Ouldhall, Bishop of Meath to threaten him with excommunication, unless within a limited time he made reparation; that restitution being refused, and Bathe continuing in his contumacy, the Bishop of Meath in accordance with the Pope's orders went in solemn procession to the market place of Navan on a market day, and there excommunicated Thomas Bathe; that after this Bathe sent some ruffians to the Abbey of Navan who forcibly carried off Dr. Stackboole to Wilkinstown, and there cut off his tongue and put his eyes out. That Dr. Stackboole was carried back to the Abbey and cast before the image of the Blessed Virgin, and by her grace and mediation and miraculous power he was restored to his sight and speech.'

A large stone cross, one of the three hundred blessed by St. Columkille formerly stood in the centre of the Market Square. It is said to have been a magnificent piece of sculpture, and standing well over twenty feet in height. On one side of it there was an inscription in Irish commemorative of the sufferings of Christ, and on another side a figure of St. Patrick. A third side had the figure of a bird perched on a shield, the arms of the Nagle family, and a fourth had the *Ecce Homo* and a crowned figure of the Blessed Virgin and Holy Child. This cross was uprooted many years ago, but a fragment still remains in a private house in Navan.

Of modern buildings the Catholic Church of St. Mary's situated in the centre of the town is a most imposing edifice. The Protestant Church too, is a very fine building looking to advantage on the eminence on which it is situated over Academy street. The new County Council Hall, erected a few years ago, is a magnificent edifice situated in a conspicuous place near the Great Northern Railway Station. The Loreto Convent is perhaps one of the finest institutions of its sort in Leinster. Its erection was suggested to a benevolent old lady, who travelling through the town was moved to pity at the sight of a number of destitute little girls who followed her carriage soliciting alms. In a few days afterwards she waited on the late Dr. Plunkett, and placed in his hands the sum of £500 towards the erection of an orphanage. This generous example was speedily followed by a large number of people in Navan and its vicinity, and with a portion of the money collected the site of the convent was purchased in 1833. A branch of the Loreto nuns was conducted from Rathfarnham, County Dublin, to the new cloisters at Navan, and since then, as well as being an orphanage, it has become a boarding school for young ladies. It has also an extensive day school, which is largely attended by the young girls of Navan.

The Round Tower and church ruins at Donaghmore

Down The River

The Seminary of Navan, founded by Dr Plunkett, was opened in 1802. Few establishments of its kind have produced such eminent men as St. Finian's of Navan. In every walk of life her students distinguished themselves, and have been proud of her as their Alma Mater. Why the people of Navan allowed this seminary to be transferred to Mullingar is something I could never understand. Yet such has been the case, and the beautiful building situate in Academy street was allowed to crumble away. A local company are about to open a picture-drome there now, for the amusement of the town folk, and at present are busily engaged preparing the building for the change. Navan just wanted something like this, as it was lacking in the way of amusement. I am sure we wish the company every success.

Passing down the river the first object demanding our attention is the round tower of Donaghmore. This tower is a fine specimen of those ancient structures which are the sphinxes of Ireland. It is 70 feet high and 12 feet in diameter at the base. Over the doorway a likeness of the Crucifixion is carven which would lead one to think that these towers are of Christian origin. But Henry O'Brien, in his book, *The Round Towers of Ireland*, endeavours to argue that these structures are as ancient as the pyramids of Egypt, and were store-houses for the idols of Buddha. He states that the figure of the Crucifixion on the towers of Donaghmore and Antrim are symbolic of the departure of Buddha. No doubt, Mr O'Brien knew something about Buddhism, but in his endeavour to people Ireland with fallen angels, and to solve the mystery of our round towers by quoting from Heccataeus, he has not achieved anything more worthy of note than Tom Thumb. Dr. Ledwidge, who was a fine authority, asserts that these were merely watch-towers of the Irish, and after the Reformation became the cupboards of the priests.

But reverting to Donaghmore and the remains of its ancient church, the true name of this place is 'Domnach-mor, Muighe

Echnach,' "The great church of the plain of Echnach." The Tripartite Life of St. Patrick relates that while the man of God was baptizing the people called Luaignii at a place where the ruins of Donaghmore now stand, he called his disciple Cassanus and committed to him the care of the church recently erected. And with a prophetic tongue predicted that he might expect that to be the place of his resurrection, and that the church committed to his care would always remain small in structure, but great and celebrated in honour and veneration. Several events have proved this prophecy to be a true one, for many remarkable miracles were performed by the relics of St. Cassanus. The church was erected in the 12th. century, and until the Reformation contingents came from all parts of Ireland to do honour to the relics of Cassanus. But all this is forgotten in Donaghmore now like an old story that was not true. Before I pass from Donaghmore I would like to relate a rather unique experience I had there.

A friend of mine wrote to me from Dublin that he had found a stone axe-head at Donaghmore, and as I would be a collector of all those things were somebody kind enough to present me with a few specimens, or fortunate enough to find some, I came from Nobber immediately to Donaghmore. I went up the old lane a few perches when my attention was drawn to an old lean cow grazing very hungrily across a gate at a field of new grass. Now I had great pity for the poor cow so I immediately threw open the gate and allowed her to pass through. I had no sooner done this when a youth raced from the other side of the field and, evicting the cow, called me a very many adjectived name not mild enough for the columns of a newspaper. I apologised and said I thought it was the cow's field and only thought to oblige somebody by opening the gate. We became friends very soon and I followed him across the field to where he was planting potatoes, and watched him work. I had a curious feeling that eyes were on me, and turning round I saw that two women were steadily watching me across the fence. I wheeled again and stooped to strike a match on a stone, when they started talking about me in this manner:

"Is he goin' to give Tommy money?"

"Money how are ye; mebbe he hasn't it for himself."

"Who is he at all?"

"He's like a peeler in disguise."

"Ye never seen a peeler wearin' specs."

"He hasn't specs."

"It's what he's one o' those Insurance fellows."

"Lookin' for John Melady; that's just it."

"Tho' it's hardly. It's more lek that fellow the Co. Council has goin' about preachin' to the farmers."

"That's who he is, and musha it's mighty aisy he earns his money."

"It'd be fitter for them devote their money to some industry that'd keep the people at home, and not be lashin' out to an idler from God knows where."

The two women waxed so vehemently that I was afraid of a physical attack from them, so I went away thinking to myself that there is often more wisdom on the tip of a woman's tongue than in the whole anatomy of a philosopher.

Pursuing the course of the river from Donaghmore towards Stackallen Castle there is a burst of beauty only rivalled by the woody windings of Beauparc. To the left a steep hill dotted with smaller hillocks hurls down a noisy little stream and the wild cherry grows there, and the woodbine and the thorn waves her flag of truce, and all is peace. Somebody fires a shot perhaps on the right, and immediately a score of little echoes repeat it round the hills, and there is a scud of rabbits from little spaces of green, and a hurry of water-hen from mid-stream to the rushy edge of the river. A lighter passes down and we hear the shout of the driver or the song of the helmsman, and the slap of the toe-rope as the strain relaxes, and the swish of the rushes as they regain their equilibrium. Here and there a tuft of whins is burning reminding one of the red tongues of Pentecost and the bush where Moses first saw God. It is savage but beautiful, an up and down of colour where bird song and water song make sweet alloy of sound. Farther down the 'Bridge of the Boyne' spans the river. A quaint bridge it is, full of triangular nooks, as if the architect was reminded that the 'Black Pig' from Ulster would come thus far, and he built those nooks as shelter for the opposing Irish. I once saw a lock-keeper, whose house is adjacent, dive from this bridge right into the canal, a drop of about forty feet. And this amphibious man saved many lives from the water, although he displays no medal nor is his name writ in any large book of the earth. A cotton mill that might give more employment than it does is situate here, and a public house where you must strike a match to find the bar. But this house of refreshment is a great acquisition to travellers, and when the pupils of your eyes dilate you will be well able to find your drink. The 'horse shoe' weir which forms the pretty picture of many a post-card is here. Continuing down the river to Beauparc the sides become more wooded and rocky and some new charm holds you mute at every bend. The river is deep and almost still for upwards of two miles here, only broken occasionally by the leap of salmon or the retreat of the bald coot. Giant trees hold out broad arms across the water and high rocks lift themselves into the tree tops carven by nature with many a grotesque face. Of these, Maiden Rock is the most beautiful. It gets its name from a story that tells of how the young girls from the innocent long ago were wont come here on May eve to play tricks and find from some superstitious practice if they would be married in the course of the year.

Directly opposite Maiden Rock is the Puck's Hole, a place avoided by the neighbouring people after dark. It is said that a puck in the form of a large dog inhabits the hole, which is a cavity in a rock, and roams through the adjacent fields at evenings; and woe betide the man or woman he meets, for he drives his body between their legs and carries them through hedges and ditches across the country. There are many stories of this puck current about here; one in particular, I remember states how he used to go to the castle yard at Slane every evening and bring away the coachman. No matter how this unfortunate would endeavour to evade him he would meet him somewhere until he became so accustomed to these rides in the dark that he would go to meet him.

Somebody to whom he related this adventure told him to wear spurs and dig them into the puck's side and he would be troubled by him no more. He accordingly did this, and the puck, roaring like an infuriated lion returned with him. But he never really got peace, as the puck always sought him, and if he was so unfortunate as to be out after dark without his spurs the puck would snap him up and leave him miles away to walk home. Another story tells that the puck used to come every night to the castle for food which would be left for him in a certain place. And once a new housekeeper came and was instructed to leave out meat and white bread for him. On hearing of this waste she said: *"Brown bread and herrings is good enough for him,"* and left this repast in its accustomed place. About the middle of that night the puck went to her room, and dragging her from her bed, flung her down the stairs saying, *"Brown bread and herrings is good enough for him; brown bread and herrings is good enough for him,"* until he flung her to the bottom of the stairs.

The ruins of Carrickdexter Castle stand close to this point at the edge of the wood. This was the ancient home of the D'Exter family, who came from France in the days of De Lacy. It is also aid that Oliver Plunkett, the Lord Baron of Louth, lived here at one time. This is most probable, as he is buried with his wife close to this place at Barristown. This tomb is a walled mound, surmounted by a cross, the arms of which are broken. It is about ten feet high. On one side, under a shield, is the 'Hail Mary,' and another prayer to the Blessed Virgin for her intercession. On the east side is a rude figure of St. Peter with the following inscription:-

'I pray you Saint Peter
pray for the soules of Oliver Plunkett,
Lord Baron of Louth,
and Dane Jennet Dowdall his wife.'

On the west side is a similar prayer and a figure of St. Patrick, and on the south side is inscribed:-

'This cross was builded by
Dame Jennet Dowdall,
late wife unto Oliver Plunkett,
Lord Baron of Louth,
for him and herself, in the yere of our Lord God'
.... (Obliterated)

Slane

'I will strike the harp with a mournful dirge
Till the glistening tears shall flow,
For that dear old land, that green old land,
Where the lovely rivers flow.'

Slane Castle, the residence of the Conyngham family, is situate on a beautiful eminence overlooking the Boyne on its northern bank. The greater portion of the present castle was erected since the Conyngham family became possessed of Slane, after the battle of the Boyne, 1690. The old castle erected by Richard Fleming after the Anglo-Norman invasion was practically destroyed during the confiscations of Cromwell.

Under the patronage of the noble family of Fleming, Slane became one of the most prosperous boroughs in Meath. In 1176, the Irish, under Melaghlin, lord of Kinel Owen, plundered Slane Castle and slew Richard Fleming. In 1414 the Irish, under O'Connor, lord of Offaly, and Mageoghegan defeated the Anglo-Irish at Killeagha, and, amongst many other persons of note, captured the Baron of Slane, for whose ransom 1,400 marks were demanded and obtained. In 1423, the same baron, with all the able men of Slane, were ordered to meet the Lord Justice at Trim to defend the English Pale. The Northern Irish, under the leadership of the O'Neills, plundered the Barony of Slane in 1595.

Slane Castle is famous for its having being visited by King George 1V in 1821, but more particularly that it was for a short time the hiding place of Dr. O'Hurley, the martyred Archbishop of Cashel, in the year 1583. It would seem that this noble prelate was denounced to the government by the spies of Elizabeth and fled to Slane Castle for refuge. He was warmly received by Thomas Fleming and his wife Katherine Preston, who was the daughter of Jenico, third Viscount Gormanston, both of whom adhered to the old faith. For the first week of the Archbishop's stay he was afraid to leave his room, but by degrees he became more confident and finally appeared at the public table, and even dined with strangers in the garb of a gentleman. On one of these occasions Sir Robert Dillon, Chief Justice, met him and the Archbishop conversed with such ease and eloquence on topical affairs that Dillon suspected he was a Catholic ecclesiastic in disguise. He communicated his suspicions to Loftus, the Protestant Primate and Chancellor. An order for his surrender with many threats was sent to Lord Fleming, but meanwhile the wily Baron became apprised of the plot in incubation and had the Archbishop transferred to Dublin. The prelate evaded the government for a short while, but was finally arrested at Carrick-on Suir, and having refused to apostatize was bound in irons, his limbs having been smeared with pitch and sulphur, and thus conveyed to Dublin, and there hanged, drawn and quartered in Stephen's Green, on the 6th. May, 1584, in the 65th. year of his age.[6]

I am telling you this, children of the Gaelic League, because it is more worthy of a page in the book of your memory than the visit of England's King. Do you remember what Byron wrote of that visit to Slane Castle:

'Ere the daughter of Brunswick lies cold in her grave
And her ashes still float to her home o'er the tide:
Lo! George the triumphant steals over the wave
To the long cherished isle which he loved like his bride.*

Tho' the chains of the Catholic clank o'er his rags,
And the castle still stands, but the Senate's no more,
And the Freedom that dwelt on her desolate crags.
Is retracing her steps from that desolate shore.'

*(He broke his beautiful Queen's heart)

I would love to have quoted the whole poem, but I am writing this under most inept circumstances in a cottage in Dundalk, where I have come to glean what the people of Muineone know about Cuchulain.

---

[6] At Gallows cross, near the corner of Fitzwilliam Street, Dublin.

The Conyngham Family

After the Battle of the Boyne the Conyngham family came into possession of Slane. I would like to say just that the most cherished inheritance of this family is to do good and be understood fully, for when it comes to praising an individual or a house whose sole objective is to alleviate the distressed and spread a new beatitude over a neighbourhood, words are but little shapes in ink that poorly express the deeper thought and the memories of a people revered for their generosity among the poor, respected for their nobility among the noble.

Creeds and classes are to them alike, no pride deters their indulgence, no narrow minded religious bigotry intercepts their charity. Today they are seen hunting with the aristocrats, tomorrow with the labourer. The Protestant church is full of their gifts, and the beautiful chalices and cruet-stands in the Catholic church were presented by them, as well as a beautiful original painting of The Crucifixion set in a gilded frame. The present Marquis and Marchioness continue their good work with the zeal of their predecessors, interested in everybody and everybody's work. Local sports and race-meetings are patronised by them, and under their directions and personal supervision many a young boy and girl have been educated in domesticity, and thus enabled to face the world strong and independent.

There are many stories of this family extant, but the principal one is that which led up to the erection of the belfry at Slane, which was the first to be erected after the Reformation and while yet the Penal Code restricting the erection of Catholic belfries was in vogue. About the year 1790 when France and England were at war, Father O' Hanlon, parish priest of Slane, was dining with a friend in a restaurant in Paris when a soldier shouted from the door, *"Does anyone here know Colonel Conyngham?"* Fr. O' Hanlon immediately Jumped up, and having spoken to a soldier was conducted before a military tribunal. It would appear that Colonel Conyngham, who was the eldest son of the Marquis then in office, was taken prisoner, and as all prisoners, except those ennobled by birth or education were shot, the young colonel was doomed to die unless evidence of his nobility was forthcoming. Father O'Hanlon, who spoke French very fluently, interceded for the prisoner, giving his family a high character for their generosity to the Irish people. The result was that the Colonel's life was spared, and he was exchanged with the English for a prisoner of similar rank. This act was long remembered by the Conyngham family, and procured for the people of Slane an indulgent landlord and for the Catholics a true friend.

On his return to Ireland, Father O' Hanlon found that the little mud-wall chapel of Slane, situated in a place now known as 'The Keeper's Quarry,' along the castle road, was completely in ruins. For some time Mass was celebrated in the Hotel yard. Meanwhile Colonel Conyngham succeeded to the barony of Slane, and amongst the first to congratulate him was Father O' Hanlon. The Baron remembered his benefactor well, and begged to be informed in what way he could make a return for having saved his life. The good priest replied that for himself he wanted nothing, but that his people were without a place of worship, and accordingly he requested permission to erect a chapel and a belfry. The site was granted immediately, and a liberal donation, but the baron experienced much difficulty in getting permission for the belfry on account of the code then in action. Through connivance, however, he got permission from the Lord Lieutenant to erect it, not on the chapel roof but a distance of about twelve feet from the walls of the chapel.

Lady Well And St. Erc's Hermitage

A little below Slane Castle in the beautiful demesne, Lady Well bubbles up. Every year on the 15th. August, thousands of people from all parts of the country gather here to drink of the water which has wrought many wonderful cures. Farther on is St Erc's Hermitage. This building is the most dilapidated ruin in the country. It is a great pity the Board of Works do not take steps to preserve what now remains from further decay. A few years ago the front door of this ruin with its beautiful architraves fell down, and what was long an object of admiration no longer exists. Inside this building there is a cave which it is supposed connected the hermitage with the College on the Hill of Slane. One can yet travel a distance of about twenty feet in it to where the passage is built up. St Ere was the first bishop consecrated by St Patrick, and was noted for his wisdom. He ruled over the teaching community of Slane Hill, and himself helped to instruct no less a personage than Dagobert, King of Austrasia.[7] A most austere life this saint led, his food for the most part consisting of eggs and herbs. He was in the habit of rising very early in the morning and before breaking his fast plunging into the river, and standing in the water up to his armpits, prayed for two hours. There is an old story which will bear retelling about St. Erc's eggs. The King of Ulster was about to give a great feast to a foreign prince and sent his heralds through Ireland to collect the choicest meats that Ireland could produce. One of these heralds came as far as St Erc's hermitage inquiring for food. St Erc's old maiden relative who sometimes visited the saint told the herald that there was nothing in the hermitage but a bowl of eggs. The herald demanded these, and despite the entreaties of the old woman carried them away. When Ere returned he had no dinner, so going down the river he prayed that there might be no food to lay before the King on the day of the great feast. It happened that three days before the arrival of the foreign prince, when great preparations were being made to fete him in the palace of Ulster's King, an old man and woman came to the stewards seeking bread. The first morsel they ate increased their height to ten feet and the second to forty, and thus they continued growing and hungry in proportion until they left not one crumb in the whole of Ulster.

---

[7] Ledwidge is here referring to the son of King Sigebert of Austrasie, a kingdom in Eastern Gaul.

Slane Castle

ii

"...And I remember all the names,
And all the swords and ancient wars. "

A little below the Hermitage of St. Ere is a sandy salmon-bed now known as the 'Bush Hole,' from the fact that a thorn tree formerly grew there. This is yet pointed out to travellers as 'Erc's Pool,' where Finn Mac Cool caught the salmon of knowledge. It may be interesting here to recall Finn Mac Cool from the buried memories of our Seannichies, and instructive to those who are interested in the revival of our grand legends. In several parts of Ireland large stones, which did not belong to the strata of the neighbourhood, have been pointed out to me as having been thrown there by Finn Mac Cool from a distance often extending over 20 miles. I would like to make it quite clear that there were two Finn Mac Cools, and that the hero with which we are at present concerned was too busy in the political warfares of Ireland to carry huge stones about on his back, depositing them here and there over the country for mere sport.

Finn Mac Cool means the 'white son of the sky,' and has become allegorical for the icebergs that floated over Ireland, when the world was under water. As it still continues in the avalanches of the Alps, large stones became embedded in the ice which, losing its gravity, became detached from the parent berg and floating towards the equator dropped here and there as it melted, the large stones which we find over the country strange in the locality. The location of these stones have been attributed to the strength of the Finn Mac Cool about whom the present story is, but that is merely a metaphor drawn from his name and very illustrative of the iceberg 'white son of the sky.'

Finn Mac Cool's father was killed at the battle of Crucha (Castleknock) and his clan scattered. But at home in her cot, among the Slieve Bloom mountains, his wife had given birth to a son, and fearing that his father's enemies would kill him, she left her home and having changed her name, and that of her baby boy, wandered for years through the counties of Munster. While accepting the hospitality of the peasantry, the boy who was then called 'Deimne' cultivated a taste for athletic sports and soon became known in the south as an expert hurler, swimmer and hunter, so that Goll, his father's enemy sent him a messenger inviting the lad to join his ranks as a soldier. Deimne's mother was greatly troubled at this lest his identity might become known and advised the lad to leave Munster. This he accordingly did, hiring himself on the road on occasions, until at last he reached the banks of the Boyne.

Now it had been prophesied that a man named Finn would catch one of the salmon of knowledge which roamed about the river seeking the nuts of their magic hazel, and a seer named Finn, in the hopes that he would be the fortunate one spent seven years fishing the pools of the Boyne, but without any success. The lad Deimne who was but then eight years old appeared, and the seer was so much captivated by his gentle appearance and wonderful physique that he engaged him as his servant. On the second day Deimne caught a speckled salmon which he showed to his master. The seer immediately recognised it as one of the salmon of wisdom, and cautioned the boy to cook it carefully, but on no account to taste it until he, himself, had eaten of it.

The lad boiled the fish observing the instructions of his master, but in doing so the water boiled over and in order to keep the salmon in the pot Deimne was obliged to press it down with his thumb. In doing so a portion of the scales adhered to his finger giving him a severe burn and in order to cool the pain he put his thumb in his mouth. The minute he did so he was filled with knowledge, so that he saw himself at the head of a mighty army conquering the 'Clan Morra' who so much oppressed the people. When the seer asked him if he had eaten of the fish Deimne told him all that happened. *"But it has been prophesied that a man named Finn would be the first to eat of the fish,"* replied the seer. Deimne then told him how his right name was Finn Mac Cool and the whole story of his life.

The seer feeling that the prophecy was fulfilled blessed the lad and sent him upon his journey.

It would be a deviation from my original intention to recount any of Finn's exploits away from the Boyne side. So we shall leave Finn recruiting his army from Donegal to Cork, and for a short while examine what authorities prove beyond doubt is the real existence of Finn. The principal support to this theory is his pedigree in the Book of Leinster, but after all his name betrays him. Finn Mac Cool 'The Son of the Sky,' 'Cool' originally spelled Cumhal is the same word as Camulus the Gaulish heaven-god identified by the Romans with Mars. And it would seem that the 'Fianna of Eirinn' moved on an equal footing with the gods, and their battles with the Lochlana were of such an extraordinary nature that our ancient historians, in some respects, could not set down their deeds as the authentic feats of mortal warriors. But against this again we must admit that we are a people inclined to exaggerate the feats of our heroes, and if Finn really existed, as there seems sufficient to prove, he was no more than a general of a 'freelance' army whose deeds became extraordinary on the lips of our ancient Seanniches.

The Village

The pleasing little village is situated on the side of two hills. For the most part it slopes with Gallows Hill towards the west, though one of its streets is on the famous hill like a pilgrim of industry who essayed to climb it, and finding the task too difficult sat down to rest and fell into a druid sleep from which it will never awaken.

Slane is asleep. I made one of my best friends by endeavouring to prove how much awake it was;[8] but that was years ago when bread and butter could appease me and I thought man lived by that alone. But when the years of discretion came and the exigencies of life began to unfold themselves the veracity of my friend's statement came home to me, and I knelt a penitent at the feet of my elders to make an act of Contrition for the artlessness of youth. There is no place in Slane for the youth; there is no place for the patriot. Green fields and silent mills and cattle are the predominating features and West Britons who ape the aristocracy like the frog in the fable. There is no branch of the Gaelic League there, no debating society, no sense of nationality. The sins of their fathers have descended to the children and there is no hope for them, no hope. But Slane is beautiful and claims to be the Bethlehem of Irish Christianity. Every inch of it is sacred ground, and tells a story of other times. In the Protestant churchyard the tomb of Rev. Mervyn Archall, rector of Slane, is to be seen. This great scholar was the author of many valuable books of information. His name is perpetuated by his *Monasticum Hibernicum* and his book on the *Peerage of Ireland*. He died on the 6th. August, 1791. And in the Catholic church the remains of 'Dean' Cogan, the distinguished author of *The Diocese of Meath, Ancient and Modern,* sleeps.

In the top corner of the fine school-house a stone, supposed to be the mitred figure of St Ere is set. This stone was taken from the college on the hill at the time the school was erected, as was also the holy water font in the chapel.

---

[8] A reference to Seaghan Mac NaMidhe, with whom Ledwidge had a prolonged and heated correspondence in the pages of the *Drogheda Independent* in 1910. They later met and became friends.

In addition to the *Annals of the Four Masters*, *The Book of Leinster*,' various state papers, and Dean Cogan, Ledwidge wanted to acknowledge the help of certain people :

'*I would like to thank those kind friends who have helped me materially, and by their encouragement to the success of these articles. To mention a few! Lady Everard, Mrs. Shaw (local schoolteacher), Mr. T.J. Hewitt, Mr. J.P. Timmon, Mr. J.Gillick, Mr. Sean Mac NaMidhe, and Mr. P.T. Mulready from far away Boston. To all the friends known and unknown to me, I find it Impossible to answer owing to pressure of work. Hoping they will all accept this slight recognition of their goodness.*'-

Francis E. Ledwidge

Selected Prose

The Wheel Of Fortune

"His is a short Lent,
who owes money to be paid at Easter"

So runs Poor Richard's axiom in the old school books. Now As I scan the thumb-marked and detached leaf bearing the above, my thoughts revert to the happy days of my childhood, when Poor Richard and all his allegories were hummed in the droning school without one single thought on the veracity of Franklin's effusion, or one simple pain to probe out the meaning of Father Abraham's veritable sermon. We only knew it was there for us to commit to our memory, or bow to the inevitable cane. Quite unconscious of its meaning it was driven into our brains, as a carpenter drives a nail. It was only when we joined hands with the world, its true meaning came home to us. For there are times in the lives of most of us when the settling of some debt, trivial or otherwise, is fixed on a seeming far distant date, and we have not the wherewith to meet. Father Time appears to have added wings to his Pegasus and leaped several weeks while we slept.

Gale day was fast approaching on the empty exchequer of Ned Mc Hugh. Ned- I would have you know- in his day was one of the snuggest farmers in the country. You might take his house for your centre, and describe a radius of three miles and you would not find within it a more compact holding than that of Ned Mc Hugh's. The twenty acres of good land over which he reigned plenipotent would do credit to any model farmer. *"Machine!"* he would say, as some neighbour told him of the latest invention in farming implements. *"System, that's my machine, and the best of it all Tommy, I'm my own machinist."* Truly, he was correct, for the systems he employed might be advantageously followed by the bigger farmers in the district. Crop followed crop in nice rotation, and not a sod on the whole twenty acres but bore its fruit. It had been whispered abroad this house was one of no mean length, though any side questions thrust in that direction found Ned wholly impenetrable. *"It's not money I want,"* he would say, *"my childher's comfort is my desire,"* and poor Ned did well for them all. He bared his arms to the strife and wrought from morning until night, year in, year out, until the avocation of the three sons wherewith he was blest, was finally settled upon.

Ned, his eldest and favourite, having evoked a desire for the priesthood was sent to college in the South of Ireland, where he was ordained five years afterwards, and came home one Spring morning to bid goodbye to his father and mother ere he set sail for a weed overgrown vineyard in an island far in the southern seas.

Thady, his second son, having literary proclivities, took to journalism. He had a berth on a provincial weekly in the North of Ireland and was making headway until a wild desire seized him to cross the sea. There, it is rumoured, he went to the bad. He wrote to his father after some time to send him *"For God's sake"* some money to bring him home. His poor father wept as he read the letter, and without one word of upbraidance sent him ten pounds to bring him home. He never wrote afterwards. Still the father never forgot him, and if you were to mention his name to him, his good points alone he would speak on; why then should we *"draw our frailties from the dread abode?"*

Felix, the youngest, and perhaps the greatest favourite of all, had no desire further than to remain home with his father and mother, but God took him ere his young heart knew aught of care, or his pure soul was blemished by the fingerprints of sin. Stoic-like, Ned bore it all, but the poor mother was less strong and fell under the weight of her cross. *"Care and cheerfulness,"* was the prescription the doctor gave Ned, and he immediately procured the elixir Care! The least hint of a desire for any article of diet was enough for him. And as for cheerfulness, he laughed and he sang, although his heart was drowning in tears, which he was too manful to weep. Yet, despite all poor Ned could do she never recovered, but went one night to join Felix- and supposed Thady- leaving the heart-broken husband to trudge along by his lone.

It took Ned a long time to recover his former self. He went about the place like one oblivious to his past. He looked upon everything with an air of nonchalance and he seldom ventured beyond the precincts of his little farm. Thanks, however, to the healing balm of time, Ned re-crossed his Rubicon, to realise he had much to do. Several minor debts he had contracted during his wife's illness had to be disposed of. His two yearling calves realised the necessary sum, and the twin pikes of hay stored in the haggard met the half year's gale, which had hung on since the days of his tribulation; so that Ned, as he said himself, *"...made a clean breast of all and faced the world again, honest, poor and alone.".*

During the years which followed it was a hard struggle to make things meet. Rent and rates were raised every year and the land less fecund. Age was telling on the strength of Ned, and 'Mistress Care' cut many a notch on his brow. The shadow of the wolf lay across the threshold, but Ned fought desperately to keep him at bay. It had been rife among the tenants of the Barnett estate that their landlord was a kind gentleman and a philanthropist. None of the tenants had ever met him, but such tidings reached them through the medium of one of their sons, who heard much of him in the city of London, where he lived. *"Nonsense!"* Said Ned, when he heard it. *"If he was all you say he is, why did he allow his agent to throw Paddy Mc Cann out on the roadside? The man that, like me and you, and our fathers before us, worked with his two bare hands to spread his banqueting board, while he himself stood Lazarus-like at his gates begging the falling crumbs."*
"Well Ned." Tommy Fitzsimons replied, *"don't you know the agent does many a thing the landlord knows nothing about. Mebbe, if he knew about Paddy Mc Cann he would reinstate him."*
And Ned replied, *"Mebbe so!"*

The climax was reached at last. The season had been the worst in the memory of the oldest inhabitant. The turnip crop had been a complete failure through dearth of rain in the early part of the season. The potatoes had been blighted early, and almost all lost. The rain fell in torrents on the hay crop and completely destroyed it. The Boyne overflowed its banks and stretched itself with a vengeance into the farm of Ned Mc Hugh. In the cataclysm, his small crop of corn was utterly ruined, and a few cocks of hay, which he managed to save, swept down the river. Powerless to stretch forth a saving hand, he looked on at the havoc which was being wrought on him. After a while the storm subsided, but its footprints lay on the whole countryside. Here, was a cornfield levelled, and here a hay crop clinging to the hedgerows. Logs of wood, etc., etc., lay on the fields giving the whole scene the appearance of a dreary ebb tide.

The climax was reached at last. So thought poor Ned, as he chancelled his exchequer, and totting up the odd shillings and half pence arrived at the grand (?) total of fifteen shillings. Fifteen shillings! And gale day five weeks away. Never since Ned took on the management of the little farm had things looked so gloomy. He had always some little store to fall back upon when the wheel of fortune ceased revolving. Now, his haggard was empty and his fields empty laid waste, and his long pose dwindled down to fifteen shillings.

True, an old horse occupied the stables, but how could he sell him? Was it not the self same animal that for years brought the happiest trio in the country to Mass? Was it not the self same animal his son, who was now in Heaven, took such a delight in? Was it not the animal which he loved himself all through his sunny days; the animal which knew him, and loved him so well, and for whose sole use he kept up the little croft at the rear of the house? And yet, was it not good to have him in such an emergency? If he held him and he was thrown out on the roadside, what good would the horse be to him? He could not bring him to the poorhouse with him! The poorhouse! Ugh! Never that! He would lie down on the roadside and die first. Such were the gloomy musings of Ned, as he sat in the flickering rays of the dingy embers watching the ghostly shadows sweep across the wall, transforming themselves into silhouettes of faces he loved long, long ago.

Thus musing, he sat far onto the night and ere he retired, determined on interviewing Mr. Smeaton, the agent, on the morrow, and after stating his predicament, ask him to allow the half year's rent to hang on for two months, feeling certain, within that time he would be able to clear up. He took a pessimistic view of how the interview would terminate and he was not disappointed.

"I cannot concede to your request," said the agent coldly. *"When the rent is due I am under orders to collect it and am not authorised as far as you have anticipated."*

"I have never asked you to make any concessions to me before, Mr Smeaton, and were it not for the severity of the season, I would not now either."

"I am aware of that, Mr. Mc Hugh, " returned the agent, *"and I am sorry for you, and that ... my sympathy... is all I can give you."*

"But I promise..."
"I am not in a position to allow any rent to hang, Mr. Mc Hugh," interrupted the agent; *if you have not the rent on gale day I can't help it."*

"But you can't take blood from a turnip , sir."
" I have not time to spare for further parley on the subject Mr. Mc Hugh, and will be obliged to you if you would understand once and for all that should the rent not be forthcoming as usual, I shall be obliged to serve you with a 'notice to quit' within fourteen days time."
So saying, the inexorable agent slammed the door in his face

Poor Ned! There was nothing for him but to part with the old horse he loved so well. He took him in from the bawn and groomed him every day until he shone like a black mirror. He lived in the very Gethsemane of misery. He would often sit in the bawn and cry bitterly as he looked on the poor aged horse he was soon to part with. and the horse, as if understanding, would go over to him and place his head on his shoulder, as if striving to soothe the sorrow of the care-worn master.

A last, the fatal morning dawned. Ned was up betimes, and having groomed the horse, set off for the fair of Drogheda, weeping sadly the while. While passing the Moate of Newgrange, he halted for a few moments as if expecting some kind of fairy to make exit therefrom and rally to his aid. But there are no fairies nowadays at least, so thought Ned, as he permitted the animal to pursue his drowsy amble.

Scarcely had he bent round the turn in the road, a hundred yards or so further on, when the good horse stood stock still. Ned, peering in the greyness of the morning, discovered a large object in the deep dyke opposite the Dowth road. He urged the animal forward, to find two men standing over a motor-car, which failed to describe the short turn of the Newgrange road. Ned inquired if he could be of any help to them; and, being answered in the affirmative, quickly trotted back to his own house, and returned after the lapse of a few minutes bearing a tether, which he attached to the springs of the car and the horse's collar, and after a few short pats on the animal's neck, succeeded in hauling the car to terra firma. The old gentleman patted the horse's neck kindly and gave Ned a hand to undo the tracings. But little he knew of the storm raging in the breast of poor Ned, whose love for the old animal increased a hundredfold in his latest achievement. Nor did he see the big tear which gathered in the old man's eye and fall down his poor withered hand.

In reply to the gentleman's enquiries, the chauffeur explained that no damage was done to the car, save the breaking of the front mud guards. The gentleman then consulted a road map, gave his directions to the chauffeur, who was seated at the steering wheel, and addressed Ned thus:

"I am not able to thank you sufficiently for the services you have rendered, my good man, and I am extremely sorry I have not any money just here; but if you would kindly give me your name and address, I will send you a little present this evening for your trouble."

"Don't mention it, your honour!" Ned replied. *"I am always ready to oblige when occasion demands, and never require payment for the same."*

"Yes, I understand," the gentleman returned. *"But it has always been a point of mine to inquire who has rendered me a favour and your noble words have made a deep impression on me, and have engendered a great desire to pursue that point, however eccentric it may seem."*

"Sir!" Returned Ned, *my motive in answering you as I have done was not meant to infer that your honour has deviated from the rules of your etiquette, but merely to show that a poor man can be an honourable man."*

"Quite right, my man, and I appreciate your motive. But your name.....?"

"Ned Mc Hugh, sir. Edward Mc Hugh, Newgrange."
"Edward Mc Hugh," sang the gentleman in surprise, *"why then, you must be a tenant of my own."*

"Why," ejaculated Ned, *"are you Sir William de Barnett?"*
"I am," replied the gentleman.

"Well", said Ned, *"it's wonderful the ways of Fate. I have been calling you in my head for the past five weeks and here now I meet you face to face."*

The gentleman laughed. *"Why, do you attribute my visit to that new-fangled force called telepathy? But tell me your complaint!"*

There and then, he unfolded his story. His former success and later tribulation, his visit to the agent and his sorrow for the animal by his side. The landlord listened to all, and when he finished Ned noticed a frown gather on his countenance and broaden into an appearance which diagnosed an inward rage.

"So that's how Smeaton has been treating you," he said, *"I have heard much of him lately and am come to see for myself. My solicitors have informed me their suspicions have been aroused quite recently- at the last audit of the books- I assure you, Mr. Mc Hugh, his days are short and few in my employ; I only regret I have not known his villainy ere this. But you go home with your horse and consider yourself sole landlord of your holding for three years. If, at the expiration of that time, the wheel of fortune turns in your favour, I will expect you to pay me as you have been doing. If not, let me know."*

Ned could not thank him enough. He walked home with a light step, and a lighter heart.

When he reached home and loosened the horse on the little croft, he laughed heartily to see the animal gallop round the field after some goat which had the audacity to trespass on his dominion. Ned did not see the 'Might versus Right' therein, but continued laughing until a tap on his shoulder called him to himself. He turned round to see a young gentleman standing behind him after alighting from a car which was standing in the bawn.

"Good morning!" said the stranger.

"Good morning!" said Ned

"What will you take for the bag of bones?" said the stranger
"I'd take your life for him," said Ned laughing.

"But seriously, will you sell him?" inquired the stranger.
"I will! Give me a thousand pounds and bring him."

"A thousand pounds be hanged!" said the stranger. *"Which of you is the older?"* .
"Neither of us were very old the day you were born," said Ned

"Come here Ben," said the stranger to the horse. The horse came to him immediately. *"See! he knows me, while my father forgets me."*

"What!" said Ned, as he keenly scrutinised the stranger's face, *"What! Is it my own son Thady?"*

"Yes father," said the stranger, *"your own son Thady, back from America, a rich man."*

My pen is far too weak to describe Ned's joy. Sufficient to say he called on his neighbours to rejoice with him, and regretted that the fatted calf had yet to be purchased and slain ere he could satisfy the craving appetite of the hunger joy swelling in his heart. He lived long to enjoy much happiness, and had the pleasure of seeing Paddy Mc Cann reinstated and a new man filling the office which had been vacated on the arrival of the landlord. His grandchildren grew around him, making companions for his old age, and when he made his final exit from the stage of life there was many a dewy eye at the curtains fall.

The old horse survived him by several months, and when he died they buried him in his own dominion. A large tuft of grass marks the spot, as if 'Big Ben' was striving to raise himself an evergreen monument.

The Dark Sisters Of Barristown

What their real names were or where they came from nobody really knew. They called them 'The Dark Sisters of Barristown' because they were so silent and never let anybody into the secret of their lives. They lived by knitting stockings and selling them in the neighbourhood. But outside, haggling for the top price of their goods, they spoke to nobody, but passed by on the shadowed side of the road like dark and secret crimes.

Once a neighbour woman thrust in a hint about their early lives, but was badly snubbed, and for the remainder of their stay in the neighbourhood the people left that side of their existence severely alone. Two of them that were in it, old and bent, their scanty grey hair always unkempt and flying like wisps of hay straight on either side of their faded bonnets. Their hands were withered and long, and there was an evil look in their eyes that the people feared. Always they went out together walking with umbrella sticks, the loose springs of which jingled as they tapped along in the shade. They never went to Mass, nor had anybody ever seen them pray; neither had the window of their tumbled down hovel ever been lighted; and among themselves the people secretly concluded that they had sold themselves early to the Power of Darkness, and that now the lease of their enchantments had run out and they only waited in despair for the call of the Evil One.

They became a proverb for silence. Once a maiden had been seen trysting with a young man, and one of her companions, taxing her on the fact said, *"She is as dark as the two sisters."* Just then, the sisters passed up in the dark, and from that day forward the girl who spoke was seen to wither away. They buried her four days afterwards and said that the hags had waked a sheaf for her, and made plans for driving them from the country, though each feared to put these into execution lest they should share the fate of Mary Hanlon. The sisters went their daily rounds composedly, nobody ever dared to venture on the subject of Mary Hanlon's death, but buying their wares from them more out of fear than necessity.

Paddy Hanlon, the brother of the deceased girl and Tom Teelan, her lover vowed to have revenge; but when Hanlon broke his legs and Teelan lost his best cow they saw the logic of their neighbours advice and left the old hags to themselves.

Two uneventful years passed by, the old hags still pursuing the unbroken tenor of their ways as silent and as dark as ever. Then it was reported that Paddy Hanlon was engaged to be married to Lizzie Conway, the daughter of a comfortable farmer in the immediate neighbourhood. The event was to take place in Spring and was the glad talk for miles around, as Hanlon was an industrious, hard working young man and comfortable; and Lizzie was likewise industrious with a tidy fortune, and a trade at her finger ends. The courtship went on as courtships have gone on since the days of Adam, and will until the world is annihilated. The usual little tiffs over trivial nothings, the make-ups, and all the et ceteras preliminary to the great contract. But one night, a month before the date arranged for the marriage, Paddy noticed that Lizzie was somewhat paler than usual, and not her accustomed spirit. She only felt a slight headache, she said, but a great uneasiness filled Paddy, for were not these the symptoms his sister showed three years previously, but four days before her death?

Aye, and Lizzie knew that too, and she might have told Paddy that she besought the dark sisters that very day to spare her for his sake, and for that of the general peace of the country; and might have told him that their reply was a curse on his father's line, and a prophecy of doom on his own. But she didn't; she only said she had a slight headache which would soon pass. Next day he heard she was unable to rise. A rage seized him. He rushed to the hovel of the sisters and thundered on the door. They were not in, or if they were they would not answer him. He raced madly down to see his withering love, and the sight of her lying there pale and wasted almost turned his head. Back he came again to his own place, and seizing a spade, returned again to the sisters hovel. Once more he thundered on the door, but they were not in yet, or if they were they would not answer him. Frantically he started digging round the house; all day he dug, and in the evening Tom Teelan came over to pacify him. But there was no peace for him, and Teelan rather than forsake him procured another spade, and both of them dug through the long night.

In the morning, news was brought to them that Lizzie had recovered. The girl herself came down to them a little later, and the old glow warm as ever on her cheeks and the blue light in her eyes radiant as of yore. Surveying the ground they had turned up during the night, they discovered three straws with pins stuck in their joints. To these they set fire, and leaving them on the dry roof of the hovel watched the whole building light up, filling the surrounding morning with one gold blaze.

The dark sisters never returned. Paddy and Lizzie were married early in April on a lovely morning full of sunshine, and song, and love. *"Do you hear the birds love?,"* he said, *"And the river, and the shouts of the happy children? Everything is happy to-day, but nothing is truly happy but me."* And she, looking in his face said, *"But me!"*

ii

Four years passed away, having blessed them with much prosperity, and a beautiful son and daughter. Their crops produced most favourably and their flocks throve apace. No cloud ever dimmed the sun of their early wedded years, and no regret came back to them from the days of their celibacy. The Dark Sisters were seldom mentioned now, partly that they were almost forgotten, and partly that the people held them in silent awe.

But one night as Hanlon and Teelan were returning from the fair of Navan in a cart, the former perceived, as he thought, from the little hill at the old monument, the sisters' house again on fire as he had seen it on that memorable morning of four years ago. He started but his companion laughed as he pointed out to him the full red moon rising between the gables of the old hovel. Hanlon appeared comforted by this, but nevertheless a fear seized him, and the coincidence struck him as the signal of more misery. Next morning he discovered that one of his best bullocks had broken his neck across a high rock at Carrick Dexter. He sent for Teelan, and secretly they buried the animal, not even mentioning it to his wife lest he disturb her peace of mind. Next day another bullock died, and that night a dreadful thing happened. Teelan, while returning from Hanlon's saw the Dark Sisters standing on their old bend on the brow of a hill. He rushed into Kelly's, a neighbouring house, and called the boys out to see. They remonstrated with him, but after a short delay followed him out, but saw nothing.

The next night Teelan, on his way to Hanlon's again saw the sisters on the hill. He rushed into Kelly's again, but once more they remonstrated with him. They followed him out, however, but saw nothing, but they heard the 'click, click' of a spade down by the old hovel. Thither they hurried to discover Paddy Hanlon again digging frantically, and raving like one demented. They gathered from him that his son had developed symptoms which preceded his sister's death, and which his wife at one time contracted. They procured spades and dug with him all night, but when morning came it was only to bring them news of the little lad's death.

Teelan's story of the sisters' return began to gain credence now, and the whole neighbourhood was thrown into confusion. But though they watched with him for three consecutive nights until midnight, none of them ever saw the sisters. Every day, something died belonging to Hanlon, until his whole flock was gone, and then the curse turned on his crops. The oats, which had just shot out, began to wither, and the meadows were full of thistles and eblan weeds. Everybody did what they could do to comfort him, but his losses were irreparable and comfort was a thing impossible to him. Somebody proposed that he should send his remaining child away somewhere for a while, and to this he acquiesced. A friend in Dublin promised to look after the little one for him, and thither she was sent. but the curse followed her, and in a week's time they brought her home in a coffin. The mother's heart nearly broke at that, and in a few weeks she lay at the portals of death, but a neighbour woman nursed her through with gentle soothing, assuring her that all their troubles were over now, essaying to comfort her with the hope that the curse would now be uplifted. As for Paddy, he roamed the fields in abstraction, or sometimes when remembering, he would be heard digging, digging, digging, round the ruins of the 'Dark Sisters" hovel. *"I'll dig the country,* " he said, *"until I find the sheaf that they buried for us,"*

Then one night after the full moon, Teelan again saw the sisters. Next day, Mrs. Hanlon died. They buried her in the little graveyard at Gernonstown. That night Paddy rushed into Kelly's shouting frantically, and seizing a fork from behind the door, rushed out. They followed him, and there on the hill were the two sisters standing on their old bend. They retreated indoors or they did not want to incur the displeasure of the witches. Nobody saw Paddy Hanlon on the next day, or the next, but on the third they found him four fields away digging, digging, digging. *"I'll dig the country,"* he said, *"until I find the sheaf that's buried for us."*

A week later he died in a lunatic asylum. The neighbourhood began to hope now that the Dark Sisters would trouble them no more, and that their power had died with Paddy Hanlon. Each of them got a mass said in their house, and blessed medals hung on their children's necks. Tom Teelan could find no comfort in his neighbours, but feared the curse would fall to his house, since he had once planned the destruction of the Dark Sisters. He never ventured outside his door after dark, and every morning he expected to find his cattle dead.

Then again, three nights after the full moon, Mick Kelly saw the sisters. The next morning he went to the priest and told him. The priest accompanied by the schoolmaster, came over the next night, and having inquired from Kelly at what time he saw the sisters, took up their stand and waited until that hour. They saw nothing and were returning when three boys followed them and told them they were only just gone when the sisters appeared. Next day, the schoolmaster came over alone and made a minute survey of the whole place; in the evening he went home and later returned with the priest. They called at Kelly's, requesting that the boys would watch with them, the schoolmaster adding, *"You will see the sisters at exactly 12.45"*.

To the minute of the hour mentioned the observers discovered the sisters on the hill. *"Now,"* said the schoolmaster, *"follow me,"* and leading the way he rushed up the hill. The priest and the boys followed quickly at his heels, and as they neared their cynosure, the forms of the sisters began to fade and in their place stood two thorn trees.

"That explains it," said the schoolmaster. *"It is only an optical delusion."*
"But if it was a delusion," said one of the boys, *"how is it, it does not always appear at the one time?"*

"It is an optical delusion," returned the schoolmaster, *"which can only take place when the moon is past the full, and at a certain point in the heavens. When the moon reaches the full it is forty-five minutes later in rising every night until the new. Therefore, the optical delusion is forty-five minutes later each night. Thus; you beheld this on the third night after the full at 11.15. The moon was then risen one hour, as the full happened at 8. This is now the fifth night after the full moon; therefore the moon rose at 11.45, and as it would take it one hour to get into the point of the heavens where it was when you were deluded, it takes place tonight at 12.45. Do you see the point?"*

"Yes," chorused the boys, *"but how do you account for the fate of Hanlon, and the likeness of the bushes to the sisters?"*
"Perhaps a coincidence," returned the schoolmaster, *"but I really think there is something in it, for there are more things in Heaven and Earth than are dreamt of in our philosophy."*

The two thorn trees may be seen on Barristown Hill yet, but it was I who called them 'The Dark Sisters,' they were so alike. I noticed their likeness to each other, one day a long time ago, as I ate my lunch between them, and I thought I would put this story round them.

A Pen Picture Of John Cassidy

Was there ever a genius taught in this school? To tot up how many times this question was put to me would be an arduous task. From the first sunny morning I made my debut in Slane National School until the evening I left it to return no more, I firmly believe I heard the question put to the class diurnally. In those far off days it was considered an enormous task to retain the answer to every question put to us, but this one never presented the least difficulty, the answer was on the tips of our tongues; and even the most woodenheaded in the school shot up a hand- eagerly boasting of knowing at least the solution to one of old Caesar's riddles and told the blank brain of the new pupil that Mr. John Cassidy, the sculptor, was the genius educated in this self same school.

We could draw up conjectures of what a sculptor was, but the 'genius' was the greatest conundrum of all; and when on one of those days we had the pleasure of feasting our eyes, we came immediately to the conclusion that a sculptor was a man who carved images in stone, a genius because of his ability to do so, but well we knew that like the strength of Samson, his secret lay in his long flowing locks and extravagant tie. This was Mr. Cassidy from the school-boys angle of observation; but those days have passed, and although some of us have spent the meantime trying to forget what was then tyrannically forced upon us, the question and answer is still fresh in our minds, engendering an inquisitiveness into the life and works of Mr. Cassidy, whose name here is ever coupled with that of John Boyle O'Reilly.

Pupils of Slane National School, circa 1906 with (L) Mr. Madden and (R) Mr. P. Healy.

From his earliest days Mr. Cassidy has displayed symptoms of the genius that was yet to make him famous. Those who knew him in his childhood will tell you that they have seen him go about his father's fields, hatless and barefoot, in a little pair of knickers supported by one suspender slung diagonally across his shoulder, but his hands were ever busy trying to carve the head of some local celebrity from a block of wood, or building clay men in his father's farmyard.

At an early age he was apprenticed to the grocery and spirit business it the White Horse Hotel, Drogheda, and it was there his 'prentice hand' produced the West Street scene of 'Kate, the Navvy' which won for him local fame. Shortly afterwards he went to the Manchester School of Art, and for some years studied painting, but finding his talents more inclined to sculpture, he took up the latter and earned for himself worldwide fame.

I had the pleasure of being introduced to him this Summer on Slane Hill, where he was endeavouring to place an old piece of sculpture in its chronological place in Irish art. We met many a day afterwards and went for long walks together. Needless to say, I found him most affable and interesting. *"Is foreign art elevating at the present day?"* I once asked him. *"No"* he replied, *"The French have made a faux pas in endeavouring to evolutionise art. The new tendency there is, to forsake the grand old method to work on, quite regardless of Nature. They pay no heed to anatomy. For such reasons I never contribute to their official organ, the 'Tendence Nouvelle.'"* I questioned him on the 'La Joconde' which was stolen from the Louvre, Paris. Writing to me of De Vinci's masterpiece, he told me he saw the painting hanging in the ill guarded Louvre, but though it was a wonderful painting he could not call it a picture.

Mr. Cassidy is at present executing a statue of King Edward V11 for Manchester. The statue when finished will be the largest bronze statue in the United Kingdom. The figure will approach 20 feet and with the pedestal, a height of 50 feet will be obtained. Mr. Cassidy has chosen to portray the King in robes of 'The Garter' and proposes to put a crown of olives round the orb, symbolizing Peace, and the winged horse of Victory on the top in lieu of the cross. The model stands 14 inches high, and is a very close likeness to his Majesty. As an intermediate stage, Mr. Cassidy will execute another model in proportion to one quarter to the completed figure, and then proceed to the full design. The work will occupy him for about two years and a half, allowing several months for the casting in the foundry.

Manchester people are quite familiar with Mr. Cassidy's works at John Ryland's Library and the City Art Gallery. It may be Interesting to know that Mr. Cassidy executed the first statue of Queen Victoria in Ireland which stands opposite the City Hall, Belfast. In the *Daily Sketch* of Oct. 5th. A fine portrait of Mr. Cassidy by the side of his model appears, but the 'Mad Nero' looking caricature under his name in Saturday's edition of the *Irish Independent* is far from being a photograph of the man whom we so much admire.

On Active Service

The Battle of The Three Sheep
by Corporal Francis Ledwidge, 10th. (Irish) Division

The ruins of the little town of Sari Gueul crumble on a hillside midway between Monastir and the Bulgarian frontier. When we entered it on that Autumn evening, of which posterity will read, children played in its quaint streets quite heedless of the doom which overshadowed it. The older women sat in their doorways spinning cotton on rocks and reels; the younger busied themselves in domestic duties singing the while, songs which I have heard are of long suffering and the struggles of a great emprise.

A little river babbled down the valley like a clutch of turkeys, and farther away sheep bells tinkled, and the voices of shepherds were heard. We had orders to apprise the people of the great danger which threatened them, and give them all assistance in packing their little belongings for the great journey which lay before them. To me this sort of work had already become hateful, and when a woman besought me in her strange tongue to spare her the sorrow of emigration I turned aside to weep for her home and the many little things which endeared it to her heart. By midnight every soul had left the little town, and we who had so many sorrows of our own lifted our heads occasionally from our work, trench-digging, to catch the last tinkle of their little flocks fading away in the dark and the distance.

At dawn I was sent out on patrol with six men and as our way lay through the little town I took the opportunity of examining more minutely the dwelling of the Serbian peasant. In doing so I came across several flag-like strips of cloth on which welcomes were printed in badly formed English characters. But the printing was faded, and the cloth was worn with the weather. I gathered from this that we had been long expected, and these decorations hung in the street until all hopes of our coming burned out in the people's hearts.

On our return to the company's head-quarters we had nothing to report but the presence of some half a dozen sheep grazing on a mountain, which is now known as 'Rocky Peak,' and the sound of a rifle fired in a gorge on the left front. The keen morning air whetted our appetites, but beyond a biscuit and a slice of bacon per man nothing remained to appease it. We had become very expert at cooking our meagre rations when time and circumstance (and Turks) permitted, and the little dole which had been meted out to us soon underwent more changes than is found in Mrs. Beeton's Cookery Book. We steeped the biscuit for ten minutes in cold water, by which time the rasher was fried; then pouring the gravy over it we had a relish known amongst us as 'Protestant Slop.' 'Protestant' because some of the boys resented it. The same recipe with the addition of jam was known as 'Catholic Spawn,' because it was universally admired. Breakfasting of this, we talked generally of our new surroundings and the Bulgar foe whom we were so soon to meet, and for the edification of the new draft which had joined us at Salonika. We rehearsed old glories of Sulva Bay and the brave deaths of our comrades at Chocolate Hill and the Anafarta ridges.

I was telling the story again (how many times have I been asked to tell that story!) of how I shot my first Turk on outpost duty when my platoon officer approached.

"Corporal Ledwidge," he said, *"I think I heard you report the presence of stray sheep in the vicinity. Wouldn't it be a good joke to capture them for dinner, as the transport hasn't yet arrived?"*

"Capital," I answered. *"A great suggestion, indeed. How shall we set about it?"* I replied.

"If the men are not too tired," he said, *"ask for ten volunteers to round them up and drive them here."*

After changing the sentries on the advanced positions I asked for volunteers to come mutton-hunting. Everybody wanted to come, but only a certain number could be spared from duty, so I selected eight men who had dared with me before, and set off.

We found that the sheep had left the place where we had seen them originally, and had wandered beyond our most advanced post. Some desultory firing had begun on the left, and occasionally mountain battery spoke in the distance. We rather expected an early scrap with the Bulgars, but had no intimation of any in the immediate neighbourhood; nevertheless precaution was necessary, so we had a consultation in view of the sheep, who were now beyond a deep ravine cropping the scant grasses on a hill which commanded its entrance and exit. The result of the consultation was that two men, the best shots, should remain here to form a covering party for the rest as they approached the sheep from two sides. I made a wide detour left with four men, the remaining three moved towards the sheep a little to the right of them with the object of frightening them towards the ravine where we were spread out to receive them.

Scarcely had we taken up our positions when I heard a low whistle, and looking away to the right, I saw one of the three men signal with his rifle that the enemy was in sight. I signalled back to retreat, but it was too late. A rifle cracked on the hill top above the sheep, and almost simultaneously the two men covering us opened a rapid fire. It was good luck that the three men on the right were in sight of us, and could communicate with us by semaphore.

I motioned them to take cover and await events. Again and again the Bulgars fired on us, we could hear the hum of their bullets as they ricocheted off the rocks in front of us, and, worse than all, the sheep stampeded, not towards us, but in the direction of the enemy. *"Bli'me, but this won't do,"* said a man beside me, *"we mustn't lose the sheep."*
"That's what they're after, too," said another.
"Well, shoot the bally sheep," I replied, *"better give to Mrs. Green than to Mr. Bulgar."*
"We came out for the sheep, and our claim is prior to either party, so we must get them," said another.

We sent ten rounds in amongst the mutton, and lo! what should happen, to our consternation and delight- two sheep toppled over and came rolling down the hill towards us. We fired again, bringing down another sheep: the remaining three disappeared over the hill. All this time the Bulgars were firing on us, but we could not induce them to show themselves for a long time. I signalled across to the three men on my right asking if they had caught a glimpse of the enemy. They had, they replied, and estimated him at almost twenty strong, probably a looting party heading for the village, many hours too late. I had formed the same opinion myself.

Once again the two men on the hill behind us opened fire, also the party on our right Then I saw a Bulgar for the first time in my life. He was leaving an unsafe position, creeping towards a rock near the top of the hill. We fired, and he toppled down as the sheep had, stone dead. Again we fired, and discovered three more; two of them got over the hill top.

Absolute silence reigned for a minute's space, in which we could hcar the sound of many voices a little distance behind. The company had come up to join in the fun.

Bang, whiz....bang, whiz, hum sang hundreds of bullets over our heads from our own men, and whiz, hum, Bulgar rifles replied from a force which we afterwards calculated to be not less than two hundred strong. One of the men on our right semaphored over that he was in communication with the company, and had just received a message telling us to remain quite still and not to fire.

Our experience in Turkey served us in the dilemma which we now boggled in; we knew exactly what was in the minds of our officers, but our duty was to procure sheep for dinner, and there, not fifty yards away, were three dead sheep. How were we to get them? Several plans evolved in our heads, but all of them were waived aside for inscrutable reasons. Then suddenly, without a word, one of my men arose and, helter-skelter, doubled off about ten yards in front to another rock. We followed him.

After a minute's rest we were up and away again and so on until we were all huddled up behind secure cover beside the sheep. A rousing cheer from our hungry comrades told us we were observed, and, looking backwards over the ravine to the next hill I saw all the company in fighting array, and knew we were safe.

They inquired with flags if anyone was hit and told us they had lost two killed and one wounded. With our jack-knives we skinned the sheep, and cut off little strips of the hind quarters, which we toasted at a fire one lighted, and ate half raw.. It was impossible to think of returning yet to the company with our burdens, so we contented ourselves with smoking, knowing the enemy could not move unseen by our comrades.

After several hours' delay, firing became less frequent from both sides, and we received a message from an officer to return. One of the men took up a sheep and darted towards the ravine. He was seen by the enemy. He fell. No, up again, and away. Down again. Hit? No, up and away, and safe in the ravine He shouted something back to us, but we could not catch his words. Another man is away with a sheep, and another.

I followed with the other men and joined them as the first battery spitted shrapnel over our heads. It was quite dark when we reached the company at last, but we secured the sheep, and that was all that mattered. We had no more peace in the Balkans after that, and never another dinner.

FRANCIS LEDWIDGE
BY PROFESSOR LEWIS CHASE
(University of Rochester, State of New York).

If it be true that those whom the gods love die young, how lavishly the divinities are bestowing their affections. Without irony, however, the world believes that young poets who are killed in war are the darlings of the gods. It believes that a certain immortality awaits those who sing sweetly and die nobly before their prime. During the past three years it has taken signal pains to do homage to four soldier-poets in particular, not to mention others less gifted or less known- Rupert Brooke, Charles Sorley, Alan Seeger, and last but not least, the peasant poet of Ireland, 'poor, bird-hearted singer of a day,' Francis Ledwidge, who was killed in action, in Flanders, on July 31, 1917.

Lord Dunsany, poet & patron of poets, discovered Ledwidge in June 1912. He advised him and sponsored his first volume, *Songs of the Fields*, which appeared in 1915; christening, as well as sponsoring, his second volume *Songs of Peace*, of 1917. He was strictly Lance-Corporal Ledwidge's 'Captain,' in the Fifth Battalion of the Royal Inniskilling Fusiliers. In not immoderate introductions of sincere praise, Lord Dunsany spoke of his protégé's qualities, hailing him as 'the poet of the blackbird' — a highly appropriate epithet; commenting on his 'easy fluency of shapely lines'; predicting that readers will turn to him as to a mirror reflecting beautiful fields, as to a still lake, rather, on a cloudless evening ; and rejoicing that Meath and the Boyne and Ireland at large had the peasant poet for whom Lord Dunsany had long been looking, for almost only among the peasants was there 'in daily use a diction worthy of poetry, as well as an imagination capable of dealing with the great and simple things that are a poet's wares. Their thoughts are in the spring time, and all their metaphors fresh.'

Ledwidge contributed to the *Saturday Review* and to the *English Review*, and before his initial volume appeared, as I recall, three poems from it — 'A Rainy Day in April,' 'The Wife of Llew,' and 'The Lost Ones'—came out in *Georgian Poetry*, 1913-1915.' It was here I ran across Ledwidge's name, and then, early in 1917, its editor, Mr. Edward Marsh, sent me a copy of *Songs of Peace*. I was first struck by a poem which now for many months I have been using in a lecture on form, comparing it in this single respect, with Burns' 'Highland Mary', and with A. Hugh Fisher's 'Her Eyes'. It is called 'A Little Boy in the Morning,' and was written about a lad who drove cows regularly past the poet's door, whistling as he went, and who died just before the war.

'He will not come, and still I wait.
He whistles at another gate
Where angels listen.   Ah, I know
He will not come, yet if I go
How shall I know he did not pass
Barefooted in the flowery grass ?

The moon leans on one silver horn
Above the silhouettes of morn,
And from their nest-sills finches whistle
Or stooping pluck the downy thistle.
How is the morn so gay and fair
Without his whistling in its air ?

The world in calling, I must go.
How shall I know he did not pass
Barefooted in the shining grass ?'

In answer to my queries concerning a lecture upon him in a course in contemporary poetry, Ledwidge, at the front, immediately took up a pad and an indelible pencil, and wrote the following extraordinary letter. It reached me on the last day of June. It is pure self revelation to a sympathetic stranger of the most intimate interests of a poet under twenty-five years of age. In it one sees, as in a mirror, not only the landscape of which his work is full, but himself — the war and the possibility of his end, his affection for his kin and for his home, his boyish pranks, his eagerness for study, his modesty towards his past accomplishment, his faith in his future. As, still stunned by the news of his death, I look upon his delicate handwriting, there seems to me to have passed from the earth a very rare and precious spirit. Lord Dunsany prophesied better than he knew when he said that all of Francis Ledwidge's future books 'lie on the knees of the gods.'

Lewis N. Chase

Lance Corporal Francis Ledwidge

Ledwidge's Reply to Lewis N. Chase

B.E.F. France

June 6th. 1917.

Professor Lewis Chase.

'Dear Sir,——Your letter of May 15th reached me this afternoon. I have to thank you for introducing my books into your University library and for the interest which you take in my poems and will endeavour to supply you with what details you require of myself and my work for the composition of your proposed lecture. You will, of course, understand that I am writing this under the most inept circumstances between my watches, for I am in the firing line and may be busy at any moment in the horrible work of war.

I am on active service since the spring of 1915, having served in the Dardanelles and the First British Expeditionary Force to Serbia, and after a brief interval at home came to France in December 1916. Some of the people who know me least imagine that I joined the Army because I knew men were struggling for higher ideals and great empires, and I could not sit idle to watch them make for me a more beautiful world. They are mistaken. I joined the British Army because she stood between Ireland and an enemy common to our civilization, and I would not have her say that she defended us while we did nothing at home but pass resolutions. I am sorry that Party Politics should ever divide our own tents but am not without hope that a new Ireland will arise from her ashes in the ruins of Dublin, like the Phoenix, with one purpose, one aim. and one ambition. I tell you this in order that you may know what it is to me to be called a British soldier, while my own country has no place amongst the nations, but the place of Cinderella.

I am of a family who were ever soldiers and poets. In the eleventh century when the Danes invaded Ireland, many of the soldiers settled in the land and became more Irish than the Irish themselves. Amongst these was the first of my ancestors. I have heard my mother say many times that the Ledwidges were once a great people in the land, and she has shown me with a sweep of her hand green hills and wide valleys where sheep are folded which still bear the marks of dead industry and, once, this was all ours.

These stories, told at my mother's doorstep in the owl's light, are the first things I remember except, perhaps, the old songs which she sang to me, so full of romance, love and sacrifice. She taught me to listen and appreciate the blackbird's song, and when I grew to love it beyond all others she said it was because I was born in a blackbird's nest and had its blood in my veins. My father died when I was two.

There were four brothers of us and three sisters. I am the second youngest. For these my mother laboured night and day, as none of us were strong enough to provide for our own wants. She never complained and even when my eldest brother advanced in strength she persisted in his regular attendance at school until he qualified at bookkeeping and left home for Dublin. This position carried a respectable salary, but one day he returned unwell and finally died, after a long struggle, on June 10, 1901.

One by one my bothers and sisters left school for the world until there were only left myself and my youngest brother and mother. I was seven years of age when my eldest brother died,[9] and though I had only been to school on occasional days I was able to read the tomb stones in a neighbouring grave-yard and had written in secret several verses which still survive. About this time I was one day punished in school for crying and that punishment ever afterwards haunted the master like an evil dream, for I was only crying over Goldsmith's 'Deserted Village,' which an advanced class had been reading aloud.

It was in this same class that I wrote my first poem, in order to win for the school a half holiday. It was on a Shrove Tuesday and the usual custom of granting the half holiday had not been announced at play time, so when the master was at his lunch I crept quietly

---

[9] In fact, he was almost 14 years old.

into the school and wrote on a slate a verse to remind him, leaving it on his desk where he must see it. I remember it yet:

> 'Our master is too old for sweet,
> Too old for children's play,
> Like Aesop's dog, that he can't eat,
> No other people may.'

This alluded to the pancakes that are always made on Shrove Tuesday and are a great treat in rural Ireland. The silly verse accomplished its end. Years afterwards he often spoke to me of that verse and wished he had the slate to present to some one who liked the story and my poetry.

There was a literary society for juveniles run through the pages of a Dublin weekly, and I soon became a member of this. In all the competitions for which I entered I carried off the prize, and soon had a decent library of the books which interest children. Odd halfpennies which I got for some message run from the neighbours accumulated in time to half-crowns which in their turns were exchanged for 'The Arabian Nights,' 'Robinson Crusoe,' 'Don Quixote,' and the poems of Keats and Longfellow. My admiration for Longfellow began early and I could recite passages from 'The Golden Legend' at eight years. I loved the series of metaphors in 'Hiawatha' beginning :

> 'Fiercely the red sun descending
> Burned his way along the mountains, etc'

but thought nothing in the world as wonderful as Shakespeare's fairy song :

> 'Full fathom five thy father lies
> Of his bones are corals made, etc'

While I was still at school many silly verses left my pen, written either for my own amusement or the amusement of my companions. Indeed I left many an exercise unfinished worrying over some thought that shaped itself into rhyme.

I have always been very quiet and bashful and a great mystery in my own place. I avoided the evening play of neighbouring children to find some secret place in a wood by the Boyne and there imagine fairy dances and hunts, fires and feasts. I saw curious shapes in shadows and clouds and loved to watch the change of the leaves and the flowers, I heard voices in the rain and the wind and strange whisperings in the waters. I loved all wandering people and things, and several times tried to become part of a gipsy caravan. I read of Troy and Nineveh, and the nomads of the East, and the mystery of Sahara. I wrote wander songs for the cuckoos and Winter songs for the robin. I hated gardens where gaudy flowers were trained in rows but loved the wild things and the free, the things of change and circumstance. Meanwhile the years were coming over me with their wisdom, and I began to realize that men cannot live by dreams. I had no more to learn in National School at fourteen so I strapped up my books and laid them away with the cobwebs and the dust. My mother apprenticed me to a Dublin grocer and sent me off one Spring morning with many tears and blessings and nothing of anything else. I could not bear brick horizons, and all my dreams were calling me home. It was there I wrote 'Behind the Closed Eye' :

'I walk the old frequented ways
That wind around the tangled braes,
I live again the sunny days
Ere I the city knew.

And scenes of old again are born,
The woodbine lassoing the thorn,
And drooping Ruth-like in the corn
The poppies weep the dew.

Above me in their hundred schools
The magpies bend their young to rules,
And like an apron full of jewels
The dewy cobweb swings.

And frisking in the stream below
The troutlets make the circles flow,
And the hungry crane doth watch them grow
As a smoker does his rings.

Above me smokes the little town,
With, its whitewashed walls and roofs of brown
And its octagon spire toned smoothly down[10]
As the holy minds within.

And wondrous impudently sweet,
Half of him passion, half conceit,
The blackbird calls adown the street
Like the piper of Hamelin.

I hear him, and I feel the lure
Drawing me back to the homely moor,
I'll go and close the mountain's door
On the city's strife and din.'

and scarcely was the last line written when I stole out through a back door, and set my face for home. I arrived home at six A.M., dusty and hungry after a weary thirty mile walk. I determined never to leave home again, so I took up any old job at all with the local farmers and was happy.

I set myself certain studies and these I pursued at night when I should be resting from a laborious day. I took a certificate of one hundred and twenty words a minute at Pitman shorthand, and soon knew Euclid as well as a man of Trinity College. I read books on logic and astronomy, and could point out the Planets and discuss on the nebulae of the Milky Way. I read and studied the poets of England from the age of Chaucer to Swinburne, turning especially to the Elizabethans and the ballads that came before the great Renaissance. I thirsted for travel and adventure, and longed to see the Italy of Shelley and the Greece of Byron. But the poems of Keats and his sad life appealed to me most.

---

[10] see cover photo, Foreword and page 87.

.I began to pick faults with Longfellow and Tennyson, and the poems of the former which had erstwhile pleased me seemed too full of colour, too full of metaphor and often too disconnected, like a picture which an artist began at one window and finished at another. Tennyson was too conventional for my taste and nearly always spoiled his work with a prologue or an epilogue full of loud bombast or conceit. Shelley was innocent of such sins and poor Keats never heard of them.

For a long time I did little but criticise and re-arrange my books, separating, as it were, the sheep from the goats. I put Longfellow and Tennyson at the back of the shelf, and gave Keats, Swinburne, Shelley and the anthologies the foremost place in the light. I burned many copybooks which contained fugitive pieces of my own because I thought it were better for them to die young and be happy than live to be reviled.

My taste, I think, became extremely acute and I was more inclined to blow warm and cold over such works as Yeats than sit to admire as I do now. I have never met Yeats, but I hope to one day for I have much to say to him. I don't think he has quite ever reached the hearts of the people and if any of his works live it will be his early poems on Maeve and Cuchulain. If you remember his earlier works you will agree with me in saying that the revisions which he made in them in later years have robbed them of much enchantment. I agree that many of his far-fetched metaphors required elucidation, but, in attempting this, he has not always been successful. Take for instance two lines which appeared in the first version of 'The Wanderings of Ossian:'

'Empty of purple hours as a beggar's cloak in the rain,
As a grass seed crushed by a pebble, or a wolf sucked under a weir.'

I always pointed out these similes as the most ludicrous of Yeats. They do not illustrate his meaning, and were probably written in a rainstorm in a moment certainly happy for rhyme, not for reason. In the revised edition it reads:
'As a haycock out on the flood, etc.'

which is better because it gives you a picture of things adrift, of loneliness and the beauty of a cataclysm. This is the single exception in his work of where his second thoughts were better than his inspiration. I am afraid Masefield is getting this bad habit also. When his 'Dauber' appeared first in The *English Review,* I was struck by a wonderful line in the kitchen scene of which Dauber spoke. His sister was dusting and,

'A wagging corner of the duster flicked...'

but when it appeared in book-form this line was replaced by another which had no thought. What a pity it is that these men won't remember that they do the Gods' work and not their own. I never revise. It is too dangerous. I can't dictate to the Gods.

Georgian Poetry, (with my three excluded) contains, I think, the best poems of the century. What could be sweeter than the Songs at the 'Gates of Damascus' (J. E. Flecker's), or Stephens' 'Great Paths?'

Of myself, I am a fast writer and very prolific. I have long silences, often for weeks, then the mood comes over me, and I must write and write no matter where I be or what the circumstances are. I do my best work in Spring. I have had many disappointments in life and many sorrows, but in my saddest moment song came to me and 1 sang. I get more pleasure from a good line than from a big cheque. Though I love music I cannot write within earshot of any instrument. I cannot carry a watch on account of the tick, real or imaginary, and might as well try to sleep under the Bell of Bruges as in a room where a clock stands. I write a lot late at night in my rooms, though mostly my poems are written out of doors.

I have been to Naples, Egypt, Greece, Serbia, Spain and France, but in no country have I found a people as wonderful or as strange as my own. I have written many short stories and one play which is declared a success by eminent playwrights who have read it. 'Rainy Day in April,' was written when 1 was once temporarily away from home. It was inspired by home-sickness and a drenching which I got on a bicycle :

'When the clouds shake their hyssops, and the rain
Like holy water falls upon the plain,
'Tis sweet to gaze upon the springing grain
And see your harvest born.

And sweet the little breeze of melody
The blackbird puffs upon the budding tree,
While the wild poppy lights upon the lea
And blazes mid the corn.

The skylark soars the freshening shower to hail,
And the meek daisy holds aloft her pail,
And Spring all radiant by the wayside pale
Sets up her rock and reel.

See how she weaves her mantle fold on fold,
Hemming the woods and carpeting the wold.
Her warp is of the green, her woof the gold,
The spinning world her wheel.'

'The Wife of Llew' was written in a meadow full of flowers and singing birds:

'And Gwydion said to Math, when it was Spring :
"Come now and let us make a wife for Llew."
And so they broke broad boughs yet moist with dew.
And in a shadow made a magic ring :
They took the violet and the meadow-sweet
To form her pretty face, and for her feet
They built a mound of daisies on a wing,
And for her voice they made a linnet sing
In the wide poppy blowing for her mouth.
And over all they chanted twenty hours.
And Llew came singing from the azure south
And bore away his wife of birds and flowers.'

'The Lost Ones,' was written in a sad mood when I remembered all whom I knew and who were lost and away for ever. I wanted some one to console me by assuring me that beyond the dark, they would meet me again :

> 'Somewhere is music from the linnets' bills,
> And thro' the sunny flowers the bee wings drone,
> And white bells of convolvulus on hills
> Of quiet May make silent ringing, blown
> Hither and thither by the wind of showers,
> And somewhere all the wandering birds have flown;
> And the brown breath of Autumn chills the flowers.
> But where are all the loves of long ago ?
>
> O little twilight ship blown up the tide,
> Where are the faces laughing in the glow
> Of morning years, the lost ones scattered wide?
> Give me your hand, 0 brother, let us go
> Crying about the dark for those who died.'

My favourites amongst my own are always changing. Of those published I, perhaps, like 'Thomas MacDonagh' best:

> 'He shall not hear the bittern cry
> In the wild sky, where he is lain,
> Nor voices of the sweeter birds
> Above the wailing of the rain.
>
> Nor shall he know when loud March blows
> Thro' slanting snows her fanfare shrill,
> Blowing to flame the golden cup
> Of many an upset daffodil.
>
> But when the Dark Cow leaves the moor,
> And pastures poor with greedy weeds,
> Perhaps he'll hear her low at morn
> Lifting her horn in pleasant meads'

Better work than any you have yet seen from me is being selected for my next book, but my best is not yet written. I mean to do something really great if I am spared, but out here **one may at any moment be hurled beyond Life**. Here is a little recent thing— 'Pan' :

'He knows the safe ways and unsafe.
And he will lead the lambs to fold,
Gathering them with his little pipe,
The gentle and the overbold.

He counts them over one by one
And leads them back by rock and steep
To grassy hills where dawn is wide
And they may run and skip and leap.
And just because he loves the lambs
He settles them for rest at noon,
And plays them on his oaten pipe
A wonder of a little tune.'

Best wishes and thanks.
  Yours very sincerely,

Francis Ledwidge

140

'I tell you this in order that you may know what it is to me to be called a British soldier, while my own country has no place amongst the nations, but the place of Cinderella.'

'The Irish Cinderella and her Haughty Sisters, Britannia and Caledonia' as a symbol of impoverished Ireland at the time of the famine- Punch, 1846.

Sources

Drogheda Independent, 1913-14: 'Legends of the Boyne'
    ibid 27/12/1913: The Dark Sisters of Barristown
    ibid   14/10/1911: A Pen Picture of John Cassidy
Irish Weekly Independent, 9/9/1911:'The Wheel of Fortune.'
Sunday Chronicle, 7/5/1916: 'The Battle of Three Sheep'
Irish Times, 31/7/04, report of lecture by Gerald Dawe
Century Magazine, 1918:vol. 95, Article by Lewis Chase
Library of Congress, Washington D.C.: Letter to Lewis Chase
Francis Ledwidge, The Poems Complete, 1997: 'The Call'
Seumas O' Kelly papers, Ms.4160, Nat. Lib. of Ireland:
                           'The Sorrow of Drumree'

Suggested Further Reading

Francis Ledwidge Poet, Activist and Soldier, The first biography in over 30 years: author, Liam O'Meara. Riposte Books, ISBN. 1901-596-133

The Best Of Francis Ledwidge, new selection of poems intro. by Ulick O'Connor and edited by L. O'Meara, ISBN. 1-901596-10-9 (both of the above available directly from the Inchicore Ledwidge Society, 43, Emmet Crescent, Inchicore Dublin 8.)

Francis Ledwidge, The Poems Complete: Goldsmith Press
Francis Ledwidge, The Life Of The Poet: Alice Curtayne,
Wonders of the Boyne Valley: Kenneth MacGowan
Slane: C.E F. Trench
The Lives Of The Irish Saints: Canon O'Hanlon
The Boyne, A Valley of Kings: Henry Boylan
Guide to the National Monuments of Ireland: P. Harbison
The Beauties of the Boyne and Blackwater: Sir. Wm. Wilde